A POPULAR ACCOUNT OF THE THUGS AND DACOITS

A POPULAR ACCOUNT OF THE THUGS AND DACOITS, THE HEREDITARY GAROTTERS AND GANG-ROBBERS OF INDIA.

BY

JAMES HUTTON

GYAN

Published by

GYAN

Gyan Publishing House
5, Ansari Road
Daryaganj, New Delhi-110002
Phone: 011-47034999, 9811692060
E-mail: books@gyanbooks.com

Distribution Network
gyanbooks.com
India, USA, Canada, UK, Australia

ISBN: 978-93-6208-702-7 (PB)
First Published, 1857

2nd Impression 2024

Printed at: Gyan Press, Delhi.

A POPULAR ACCOUNT OF THE THUGS AND DACOITS
Author: JAMES HUTTON

A
POPULAR ACCOUNT
OF THE
THUGS AND DACOITS

A POPULAR ACCOUNT OF THE THUGS AND DACOITS, THE HEREDITARY GAROTTERS AND GANG-ROBBERS OF INDIA.

BY

JAMES HUTTON.

LONDON:
WM. H. ALLEN AND CO., 7, LEADENHALL STREET.
1857.

Thugs and Thuggee.

They who reverence ancient descent, and a long line of ancestors, are bound to regard the Thugs with peculiar veneration. Perhaps, neither in Asia nor in Europe are there any other families that can date their origin from such remote antiquity. They are said to be sprung from the Sagartii, who contributed 8,000 horse to the army of Xerxes, and are thus described by Herodotus, in the Seventh Book of his History:—

"These people lead a pastoral life, were originally of Persian descent, and use the Persian language; their dress is something betwixt the Persian and the Pactyan; they have no offensive weapons, either of iron or brass, except their daggers; their principal dependence in action is on cords, made of twisted leather, which they use in this manner: when they engage an enemy, they throw out these cords, having a noose at the extremity: if they entangle in these either horse or man, they without difficulty put them to death."

There is some reason to believe, that in later times the descendants of these Sagartii accompanied one of the Mahommedan invaders of India, and settled in the neighbourhood of Delhi. In the latter part of the seventeenth century, Thevenot makes mention of a strange denomination of robbers, who infested the road between that city and Agra, and used "a certain rope, with a running noose, which they can cast with so much sleight about a man's neck, when they are within reach of him, that they never fail, so that they strangle him in a trice." These vagrant plunderers were divided into seven clans or families, called Bahleem, Bhyns, Bhursote, Kachunee, Huttar, Ganoo, and Tundil, the parent stock of all the subsequent ramifications. According to tradition, they were expelled from Delhi by one of the emperors of the house of Gouree, on account of the murder of a favourite slave. Their victim had long been aware of their practices, and had connived at them, for the sake of the handsome gratuities presented as the price of his silence. But, abusing his power, and making exorbitant demands, he quickly experienced the fate of those in whose plunder he had so freely participated.

The murderers were therefore driven from the neighbourhood, after being branded on their posteriors with the current copper coin of the empire. Five of the clans removed to Agra, whence their descendants were afterwards called Agureea. A large body of them appear to have travelled to Arcot, and there founded the proudest and most punctilious branch of the fraternity. These Arcottee Thugs used to wear checkered *loongees*, and short jackets, like the Company's Sepoys; they also carried a knapsack on their back, a light cane in their hand, and generally a small bag of beetel nut and paun. Their leaders, or jemadars, frequently assumed the garb and bearing of wealthy merchants, and had four or five attendants to cook for them, hand the hookah, clean their pony, and do other menial offices, while the rest of the gang followed in small parties, not to excite suspicion, but closed up rapidly when the signal was passed along. The true Hindostanee Thugs, however, professed to look down upon those of Arcot, and refused to intermarry with them. The latter retorted, that the others could have no pretensions to high birth, for at their marriages the matrons, as they threw down the *toolsee*, were wont to exclaim, "Here's to the spirits of those (Qulunders), who once led bears and monkeys; to those who drove bullocks, and marked with the *godnee* (kunjurs, or gipsies); and to those who made baskets for the head." But this was explained by the necessity of assuming disguises, in the first place, to escape from Delhi, and afterwards for carrying on their terrible vocation. There was certainly one very low Hindoo class, the *Sooseeas*, but calling themselves *Nacks* and *Thories*, with whom the others associated with reluctance. These chiefly confined themselves to Malwa and Rajpootana, travelling as merchants, with their leader indulging in a hackery or palanquin. Sometimes they disguised themselves as Sepoys, or as treasure-bearers. The most exclusive clan were the Chingurees, or Mooltanee Thugs, who practised female infanticide to a frightful extent. They preserved alive only a sufficient number to provide wives for the members of their own clan. They were allowed to be an ancient tribe, and were much respected by the inferior associations with whom they had nothing in common, except the dialect peculiar to all Thugs. They usually travelled with their families as Brinjarees, with bullocks and cows laden with goods, and strangled their victims with a bullock's rope. A colony of about one hundred families was settled at Hingolee.

A very clever and staunch tribe, known as the Jumaldehee Thugs, settled in Oude, who prudently kept their wives in ignorance of the true nature of their pursuits, nor did they initiate their sons till they had reached the age of puberty. When they sallied forth on their expeditions, they left a certain number of their men at home, to take care of the women and children, and to these they allotted a full share of their spoils. The Brinjaree Thugs were especially fortunate in escaping detection, or even suspicion, by reason of their nomade habits, which rendered it extremely difficult to trace any particular crime to them. They were consequently enabled to amass considerable riches, though they seldom renounced their wandering life. A Thug approver told the late Major-General Sleeman, that on one occasion he and his party fell in with a company of merchants from the westward, who were encamped near Jyepore, and wore exceedingly high turbans. "What enormous turbans these men wear!" he remarked to a comrade, using their slang term, *aghasee.* The chief man among the strangers thereupon stepped forward, and requested the travellers to sit down with them, adding, at the same time, "My good friends, we are of your fraternity, though our *aghasees* are not the same." It turned out that these supposed merchants were a gang of Brinjaree Thugs, who, having become wealthy, had given up strangulation, but were not the less glad to welcome those who still laboured at the pious crime.

In the beginning, as already stated, the Thugs were invariably followers of the Prophet, but after a time Hindoos were initiated, who inoculated their Mussulmaun teachers with their own superstitions. Thuggee now became a divine institution, ordained by the goddess Kalee. It is curious to observe how the amalgamation of the two religions took place. Captain Sleeman asked a Thug approver, named Sahib, if he thought the English would ever succeed in suppressing Thuggee? The answer was, "How can the hand of man do away with the works of God?"

SLEEMAN.—You are a Mussulmaun?

SAHIB.—Yes; and the greater part of the Thugs of the south are Mussulmauns.

SLEEMAN.—And you still marry, inherit, pray, eat, and drink, according to the Koran? and your Paradise is to be the Paradise promised by Mahommed?

SAHIB.—Yes. All, all.

SLEEMAN.—Has Bhowanee been anywhere named in the Koran?

SAHIB.—Nowhere.

It was then explained that Bhowanee was supposed to be another name for Fatima, daughter of the Prophet, and wife of Ali. Sahib acknowledged that Bhowanee had no power to admit her votaries into Paradise, nor any influence over the future state, but maintained that she directed the destinies of Thugs in this world, and that God would never punish any one for obedience to her commands. Sleeman's Mahommedan officers indignantly protested against the idea that Fatima and the Hindoo goddess were identical, and professed an entire disbelief in the divinity of Kalee. But they were somewhat disconcerted when the Thugs asked how they reconciled this want of faith with their presence at Kalee's festivals: they could not say that they were merely spectators, led thither by an idle curiosity. The Thugs then adduced, as a proof of the divine origin of their calling, the fact that they had pursued it with impunity for nearly two centuries. Captain Sleeman having declared that neither he nor his native officers cared one jot for their goddess, and that they were determined to put down her worship in this form, one of them replied, "They may say so, but they all know that no man's family can survive a murder committed in any other way; and yet Thugs have thrived through a long series of generations. We have all children like other men, and we are never visited with any extraordinary affliction."

It may be here parenthetically stated, that of the Oude Thugs nine-tenths were Mahommedans; in the Doab, one-fifth; south of the Nerbudda, three-fourths; in Rajpootana, one fourth; and in Bengal, Behar, Orissa, Bundlecund and Saugor, about one-half.

Kalee, the goddess who presided over Thuggee, was worshipped also under the names of Bhowanee, Devey, and Davey. She was the wife of Mahadeo, or Siva, and first appeared on earth on the banks of the Hooghly, at a spot afterwards called, in memory of the event, Kalee Ghaut, now Calcutta. Here stands her most honoured temple, and here is still celebrated with the most solemn rites her chief festival, the Doorga Pooja. They who address her with the greatest reverence style her Kunkalee, or the "man-eater," and represent her as quaffing huge draughts of blood from men and demons. When alone, she is depicted as black and hideous of aspect; but in company with her husband, she is ever fair and beautiful. Once on a time the world was infested with a monstrous demon named Rukut Beej-dana, who devoured mankind as fast as they were created. So gigantic was his stature, that the deepest pools of the ocean reached no higher than his waist. This horrid prodigy Kalee cut in twain with her resistless sword, but from every drop of blood that fell to the ground there sprung up a new demon. For some time she went on destroying them, till the hellish brood multiplied so fast that she waxed hot and weary with her endless task. So she paused for a while, and from the sweat, brushed off one of her arms, she created two men, to whom she gave a *roomal*, or handkerchief, and commanded them to strangle the demons. When they had slain them all, they offered to return the *roomal*, but the goddess bade them keep it and transmit it to their posterity, with the injunction to destroy all men who were not of their kindred. There were many exemptions, however, from this rule. The murder of women, for instance, was positively prohibited, and this prohibition was seldom or never violated in Bengal, Behar, or Orissa. To the south of the Nerbudda old women did not always escape, or even young women, when it was found impossible to separate them from a tempting prize. Between the Nerbudda, the Indus, and the Jumna, the Thugs had few scruples of any kind. It was likewise unlawful to murder a Brahman or a Kaet (member of the writer caste), or a religious mendicant of any kind, or oilman, potter, carpenter, blacksmith, goldsmith, elephant-driver, musician, dancing-master, or any one having a domestic animal with him, or carrying a parent's bones to the sacred river. But, in later times, these restrictions were either totally evaded or confined to the first day of the expedition. To the neglect of these and such-like regulations, the approvers ascribed the decay of the "time-honoured craft." Davey used to protect them, they said with a sigh, when they "had some regard for religion." She never forsook them till they neglected her. They were merely instruments in the hands of God. "No man is ever killed by man's killing," but through the will of the Deity. Many "incursions" had been made at different times against Thuggee, but never on such a scale as that instituted by the company's officers. "The Company's Ikbal (genius, or good fortune) is such, that before the sound of your drums, sorcerers, witches, and demons take flight, and how can Thuggee stand?" In the early ages of the "institution," Bhowanee used to dispose of the dead bodies and efface all signs of the murder, but she distinctly warned her votaries against looking back after they had again taken to the road. Curiosity, however, at length proved too strong for the sons of Eve, and one day it came to pass that a Thug looked over his shoulder and beheld the goddess playing at ball with the corpses, throwing them up into the air and catching them as they fell; or, according to another account, she had a dead body in her mouth, the extremities projecting on either side. After this discovery of her favourite pastimes, Kalee refused to have anything more to do with their victims, and left it to themselves to conceal the tokens of their "piety." But she did not altogether abandon them. Even in her wrath she was gracious to those who held her name in honour. She accordingly bestowed upon them one of her teeth for a pick-axe, a rib for a knife, and the hem of her garment for a noose: yellow and white being the colours she most affected, such were frequently the hues of the *roomal*. To the last she "everywhere protected the Thugs, so long as they attended religiously to their duties." Even when through inattention to the omens she sent for their guidance, any of them were apprehended and punished, her vengeance was sure to overtake their oppressors. "Was not Nanha," said an approver, "the Raja of Jhalone, made leprous by Davey for putting to death Bodhoo and his brother Khumoolee two of the most noted Thugs of their day? He had them trampled under the feet of elephants, but the leprosy broke out upon his body the very next day." Nanha was so sensible of his guiltiness, that he did all in his power to appease Davey. "Bodhoo had begun a well in Jhalone; the Raja built it up in a magnificent style; he had a Chubootra (tomb) raised to their name, fed Brahmans, consecrated it, had worship instituted upon it, but all in vain; the disease was incurable, and the Raja died in a few months a miserable death. . . . . . When Madhajee Scindiah caused seventy Thugs to be executed at Mathura, was he not warned in a dream by Davey that he should release them? And did he not, the very day after their execution, begin to spit blood? And did he not die within three months? . . . . . When Dureear, the Rathore, and Komere and Patore, the Kuchwaha Rajpoots, Zemindars, arrested eighty of the Thugs who had settled at Nodha, after the murder of Lieutenant Monsell, they had many warnings to let them go, but they persisted and kept them till some thirty died. They collected 10,000 rupees, at the rate of 125 rupees from every Thug. What became of their families? Have they not all perished? They have not a child left. Rao Sing Havildar, the Gwalior Soobah of Nodha, took the money, but that very day his only son and the best horse in his stable died, and he was himself taken ill and died soon after a miserable death. . . . . The Raja of Kundul, some ninety coss (180 miles) east from Hyderabad, arrested all the Thugs in his Raj for some murders they had committed. For three successive nights the voice of Davey was heard from the top of every temple in the capital, warning the Raja to release them. The whole town heard her, and urged the Raja to comply. He was obstinate, and the third night the bed on which he and his Ranee were sleeping was taken up by Davey, and dashed violently against the ground." They were dreadfully bruised and frightened, and lost no time in releasing their heaven-protected prisoners.

Kalee not only protected the Thugs, but sent them numerous omens as encouragement or warning. An omen was, in fact, a positive command to slay the travellers in their power, or to allow them to go unharmed. If they did not attend to these omens, they became guilty of disobedience, and had no longer any claim upon the goddess for protection. On Captain Sleeman inquiring if any evil would befall them if they used the *roomal* without reference to the divine signals, Sahib at once answered in the affirmative, adding, "No man's family ever survives a murder: it becomes extinct. A Thug who murders in this way loses the children he has, and is never blessed with more. He cannot escape punishment." "But how," said Captain Sleeman, "how can you murder old men and young children without some emotions of pity—calmly and deliberately as they sit with you and converse with you, and tell you of their private affairs—of their hopes and fears—and of the wives and children they are going to meet after years of absence, toil, and suffering?" The answer was such as might almost have been made by an ancient Hebrew, had any one asked him if he felt no pity for the wretched Canaanites he so ruthlessly murdered. "From the time that the omens have been favourable, we consider them as victims thrown into our hands by the Deity to be killed; and that we are the mere instrument in her hands to destroy them: that if we do not kill them, she will never be again propitious to us, and we and our families will be involved in misery and want." In precisely such a spirit did Samuel hew in pieces before the Lord, Agag, king of the Amalekites. The Thugs were by no means insensible to domestic feelings, or even to the charms of social and friendly intercourse. At home their conduct was irreproachable. Their villages were usually models of cleanliness and neatness; their lands were industriously cultivated, their wives and children treated with all kindness and affection. When Laek, an approver, heard of his brother's arrest, he repeated with much feeling an Hindustani verse, which has been thus rendered into English:—"I was a pearl, once residing in comfort in the ocean. I surrendered myself, believing I should repose in peace on the bosom of some fair damsel—but, alas! they have pierced me and passed a string through my body, and have left me to dangle in constant pain as an ornament to her nose." Their wives frequently were quite unconscious that their husbands were murderers, though they may perchance have suspected them of being thieves and robbers. The sons also were kept in ignorance of the entire truth until they had completed their fourteenth or fifteenth year. In fact, they were gradually trained to the business. At first they were taken out as if for a pleasant excursion, and had generally a poney to ride. Presents, too, were given them after each murder, though they were not made acquainted with the source whence those gifts were derived. However, before they returned home they had usually a shrewd suspicion that their treasured prize had not been honestly come by. Next year they were plainly told that their parents and relations were highway robbers; but by this time they had become too fond of the careless roving life and of their share of the easily-acquired plunder, to listen to the still small voice of conscience. And thus in the third year they were not horrified to learn that they were accomplices in murder. By such gentle transitions the best regulated mind may eventually be attuned to the most atrocious guilt. A comical reason was given to Captain Sleeman to account for the omission on the part of a Thug father to initiate his son. "His father," said the witness, "used to drink very hard, and in his fits of intoxication he used to neglect his prayers and his days of fast. All days were the same with him. This lad, Shumshera, was always sober and religiously disposed, and separated from his father, living always with his uncle Dondee, who was a very worthy, good man." He, too, was a Thug, but likewise refrained from removing the veil from the eyes of the lad. Another relative, however, proved less considerate, and flattered the young man's vanity by telling him that he belonged to a very high family of the Jumaldehee Thugs. A sad tale concerning another youngster was related by Feringeea, a noted leader, who turned king's evidence. One Aman Soobahdar went out upon an expedition, accompanied by his cousin Kurhora, aged scarcely fourteen, whom he gave in charge to Hursooka, his adopted son. After a time the gang fell in with a party of five Sikhs, whereupon Aman desired Hursooka to keep the boy well in the rear, so that he might not witness the contemplated murder. Kurhora, however, becoming frightened, broke away from his companion and galloped to the front to overtake the others. Just as he came in sight, the signal was given. In an instant the fatal noose was applied, a few shrill cries rent the air, and five writhing human bodies lay convulsively distorted on the ground. At the horrid spectacle Kurhora "was seized with a trembling, and fell from his pony; he became immediately delirious, was dreadfully alarmed at the sight of the turbans of the murdered men, and when any one touched or spoke to him, talked about the murders and screamed exactly like a boy talks in his sleep, and trembled violently if any one spoke to him or touched him." Three or four of the party remained with the poor lad, for he was a great favourite with them all, but he never recovered his senses, and died before the evening. Hursooka took his death so much to heart that he retired from the world, turned Byragee (an ascetic), and passed the remainder of his days in serving at a temple on the Nerbudda.

Feringeea, the narrator of the preceding mournful incident, was a fine handsome fellow, greatly admired by the women, and much respected by his associates. His name was given to him in memory of an attack made by a party of Feringees (Europeans) under the French General Perron, on his uncle's village in distraint of certain customs' dues. As his mother fled from the scene of violence and brutality, she was seized with labour pains and brought a man child into the world, whom, in remembrance of the terror and anguish she had endured, she named Feringeea. On one occasion Feringeea, when he had grown to man's estate and had become a famous leader, was travelling with his cousin Aman Soobahdar and a gang of 150 Thugs through Rajpootana, when he fell in with a handmaid of the Peishwah Bajee Rao, on her way from Poonah to Cawnpore. "We intended to kill her and her followers," he quietly remarked to Captain Sleeman, "but we found her very beautiful, and after having her and her party three days within our grasp, and knowing that they had £15,000 worth of property in jewels and other things with them, we let her and all her party go; we had talked to her and felt love towards her, for she was very beautiful."

But beauty was not always equally powerful to save. At another time, he came up with a beautiful young Moghulanee, travelling with an old female servant, mounted on a pony, an armed attendant, and six palanquin-bearers. The ill-fated damsel, unhappily for herself and her companions, became enamoured of the dashing, handsome young Thug. In vain he tried to shake her off, for he feared a scandal might arise if he, a Brahmin, had any improper intercourse with a Mussulmaunee. And the exchange of other than Platonic love would have saved her life. So at last he insisted that they should "take" her, and she was accordingly put to death. "It was her fate," he said, not excusing himself, but putting the matter in the right light, "It was her fate to die by our hands." Captain Sleeman, then asked Madar Buksh, who actually strangled the poor Moghulanee, if he had no pity for the beautiful young woman. "I had," he answered, "but I had undertaken the duty, and we must all have food." As if hurt by the enunciation of such a base practical motive, Feringeea here struck in, saying, "We all feel pity sometimes, but the *goor* (consecrated coarse sugar) of the Tapoonee, (feast after a murder), changes our nature. It would change the nature of a horse. Let any man once taste of that *goor*, and he will be a Thug, though he knew all the trades and have all the wealth in the world. I never wanted food; my mother's family was opulent, her relations high in office: I have been high in office myself, and become so great a favourite wherever I went, that I was sure of promotion; yet I was always miserable while absent from my gang, and obliged to return to Thuggee. My father made me taste of that fatal *goor* when I was yet a mere boy; and, if I were to live a thousand years, I should never be able to follow any other trade." The fascination of the abominable "trade" is almost incredible. There were many instances of Thugs enlisting into the Company's service, and making excellent soldiers; and yet, whenever an opportunity presented itself, they would get two parades' leave, join some of their old associates, commit as many murders as possible, and then, with satisfied feelings, return to their duty.

Feringeea, after the apprehension of his gang, could have escaped to other clans in Rajpootana and Telingana, "but," said he, "you had secured my mother, wife, and child: I could not forsake them—was always inquiring after them, and affording my pursuers the means of tracing me. I knew not what indignities my wife and mother might suffer. Could I have felt secure that they would suffer none, I should not have been taken." He was finally captured by two striplings, whom he could easily have overpowered, had he not imagined that they were supported by a party of police outside the hut, and that all resistance was therefore idle. At one period of his life, he was in General Ochterlony's service, and a great favourite with Sir David. His wife was not aware that he was a Thug. "Her family," he proudly remarked to Captain Sleeman, "are of the aristocracy of Jhansee and Sumtur, as you may know." His foster-brother, being informed the day before his execution, that his foster-mother had been arrested, earnestly begged, as a last favour, that he might have an interview with her as she was led to the scaffold. His request being granted, " he fell at the old woman's feet, and begged she would release him from the obligations of the milk with which she had nourished him, and the care with which she had cherished him from infancy, as he was about to die before he could fulfil any of them. She placed her hands on his head, and he knelt, and she said she forgave him all, and bid him die like a man." The sons were worthy of such mothers, heroic in their firm resolve. There is likewise on record one example of a woman, named Baroonee, who used to assist her husband to strangle his victims. Once she saved his life when nearly overpowered, by tightly pulling the *roomal* round the neck of the struggling wretch, till he fell dead at her feet. Mothers frequently compelled their sons to go on Thuggee, and wives their husbands; and there was one woman in the Deccan, who kept a gang, though it does not appear that she ever accompanied them. Among the ancient male leaders none was more venerated than Dada

Dheera, of the Bhursote clan, whose name was oft-times invoked over spiritual potations, at certain religious ceremonies. Next to him, was the Mooltanee leader, Jhora Naek, who, assisted only by his servant, Koduk Bunwaree, once strangled a man possessed of property to the value of £16,200. Instead of appropriating this valuable prize, he drove the mule home, assembled his neighbours, and distributed to each the share to which he would have been entitled had he been actually present at the murder. For this remarkable display of honour and self-denial, both he and his wife were canonized. The leadership was usually the reward of merit. "A man," said one of them, "who has always at command the means of advancing a month or two's subsistence to a gang, will be called a Jemadar; a strong, resolute man, whose ancestors have been for many generations Thugs, will soon get the title; or a very wise man, whose advice in difficult cases has weight with the gang; one who has influence over local authorities, or the native officers of courts of justice; a man of handsome appearance and high bearing, who can feign the man of rank well—all these things enable a man to get around him a few who will consent to give him the fees and title of Jemadar; but it requires very high and numerous qualifications to gain a man the title of Soobahdar."

It is now time to consider what omens were good, what bad, in the eyes of this strange fraternity. There does not seem to have been any particular reason for deciding on the hidden meaning of the incidents that were supposed to be sent to regulate their conduct. The division of tokens and prodigies into auspicious and adverse was, indeed, most arbitrary and capricious, and can scarcely in any one instance be accounted for. The good were not so numerous as the bad, for even these habitual murderers gladly clutched at any excuse for evading the necessity of taking human life. Very promising was it, on first setting out, to meet a woman, carrying on her head a pitcher full of water: they then felt assured of a happy return to their homes, especially if she happened to be with child. Still better was it to hear an ass bray on the left hand, and then on the right; the expedition might last for years, it would always be attended with success; it passed into a proverb—*Sou puk, heroo ek dunteroo,*—"One ass is worth a hundred birds." Another proverb,—*Bacan geedee sona leedee*, intimated, that "a jackal, crossing from right to left, brings gold." To rhymed sayings of this kind they were partial, as an assistant to memory. Here is a more elaborate instance:

> Ratee bolee teetura,
> Din ko bolee seear,
> Tuj chulee wa deysra,
> Nuheen puree achanuk dhar.

That is, being interpreted, "If the partridge call at night, or the jackal during the day, quit that country, or you will be seized." Immediate and valuable booty might be expected, if the large hill-crow were heard croaking on a tree, with a river or tank in sight; but the reverse was the case, if the bird were seated on a live buffalo or pig, or on the skeleton of any dead animal. Pleasant, too, was the prospect, if a cat came prowling to their encampment by night; and equally cheering to see a wolf, or a shrike, crossing the road from the right to the left; or a large male antelope, or a herd of small deer, or the blue jay, crossing from left to right. It was good to hear the hare calling at night, upon the left, or the loud, continued hooting of the small owl, when sitting; or the call of the partridge, on the left, while travelling, and on the right, while halting. If a herd of deer came in sight, they looked, ere long, to fall in with another gang of Thugs. The call of the sarus was the most variable of all. It was very encouraging if heard first on the left, and then on the right, on opening an expedition, and also on reaching a stage, if heard on the right; if repeated on the left, a rich prize was at hand, but ill luck was betokened if it first sounded on the left; equally inauspicious was the cry heard on the right, on leaving a stage, unless preceded on the left. The most frequent reference was to Pilhaoo and Thibaoo; by the former was meant the voice or appearance of omen-endowed animals on the left hand, by the latter, that on the right. If the Pilhaoo were good, it was improved by being followed by the Thibaoo; if evil, the danger was in like manner diminished. Unless both were obtained before setting out, the expedition was deferred to a later season. On leaving a stage, the Pilhaoo was full of promise,—the Thibaoo of warning; a rule that was reversed on reaching a halting ground.

On the other hand, if a turban fell off, or caught fire, the gang returned home, if at no great distance, and remained quiet for seven days; otherwise, they offered up *goor* (coarse sugar), and the owner of the turban alone retraced his steps. An expedition had also to be re-commenced, if on the first day or night it encountered the Ansootare, literally, "tear drops;" that is, a shower of rain falling in the dry season, or in any month save June, July, August, and September; nor could any success be anticipated if it thundered, with little or no rain, when a gang was ready to set out. A very dreadful omen was the cry of the kite, heard during the interval between the first watch and day-break. All would then start to their feet, and betake themselves to hurried flight; though no alarm was entertained if the cry were heard between sunset and the end of the first watch, because then "the omen was suffocated under their sides as they turned in their sleep." Hardly less disastrous was a lizard falling upon a Thug; any garment that it touched must be given away in charity. Nothing but ill luck followed the meeting a maimed person, or an oil-vender, or a woman bearing an empty water-jar, or a leper, or any one emaciated by sickness; to meet a donkey face to face, was called Mataphore, or "the head-breaker." It was of evil import to see a jackal, or a wolf, cross the road from left to right, or a large male antelope, or small deer, from right to left. If a snake crossed either behind or in front of the gang, they must kill it or return home; in either cases sacrifices were required. The sight of two jackals crossing the road together, in front, foretold prison and chains. The call of one jackal was bad; the general clamour, or "lamentation" of a pack, still worse; but the short, broken cry of that animal, or the noise of several fighting, rendered it necessary to take to precipitate flight. It was ill-omened to hear the call of the kite while flying, or that mournful sound known as the "weeping" of the wolf, or the low hooting of the small owl, repeated two or three times; or the loud responsive cry of two large owls, or the low clicking sound of that bird, or the slight chirp of the small owl, either sitting or flying. If any member of the gang sneezed, either on first setting out, or on leaving a halting-ground, expiatory sacrifices were offered, and all travellers then in their power were allowed to escape. Were a dog seen to shake its head, no Thug would dream of executing any design he might previously have formed.

It was also unlucky to hear cats fighting in the day-time, or after the first watch at night; or the low gurgling of the large owl, which somewhat resembles the bubbling of a hookah. If this sound were observed on first setting out, the expedition was postponed for several days; if, afterwards, on the left, the gang hurried on, for there was danger behind; if on the right, they halted, for there was danger before them. But probably, no omen was more dreaded than the sight, or the cry, of a hare. Unless a sacrifice was immediately offered, they were certain to perish miserably in the jungles, and the wild animals of the forest would drink water out of their skulls: should they impiously plunder any traveller then with them, they would obtain no booty. One of the most intelligent approvers ascribed his apprehension on one occasion to his neglect of this omen. "A hare crossed the road," he said, "we disregarded the omen—though the hare actually screamed in crossing—and went on." On the following day he and seventeen of his associates were arrested, and only obtained their release after a long detention.

It has been already stated that the Thugs attributed their recent misfortunes to their want of "religion" in neglecting omens, and disregarding the restrictions assigned to their homicidal duties. Their evasions of the latter were sometimes humorous. They were forbidden to destroy any one accompanied by a woman or a cow. But a party of fourteen, possessing both these safeguards, once fell into the hands of a gang at Kotree, in Huttah, and were persuaded by the Thugs to sell the cow to them, as they had made a vow to present one to the Brahmans at Shahpore. They did actually fulfil their pretended vow, but not until they had strangled, without any remaining compunction, every one of their unsuspecting victims, not even excepting the female. According to the approvers, the practice of killing women had prevailed only five years, and became one great cause of their ruin. The principal reluctance to woman-slaughter was entertained by the Hindoos—the Mussulmauns, perhaps, from their larger experience of the sex, showing little inclination to spare them. On a certain occasion a Hindoo lady, called the Kalee Beebee, was met by a gang as she travelled in a dooly (a sort of litter), accompanied by twelve dependents. The Thugs having discovered that she had £400 worth of property with her, her death was insisted upon by the Mussulmauns, and as strenuously objected to by the Hindoos. Thereupon a violent quarrel arose between them, which was only appeased by the former perpetrating the deed by themselves. The Hindoos, however, did not refuse to share in the plunder, save only the lady's personal ornaments and clothes. One of them, a Brahman, named Purusram, was shunned by his own brother until he expiated his guilt by feasting several hundred Brahmans at a great expense. Another member of the gang, also a Brahman, "got worms in his body, and died barking like a dog." A third died miserably, and the families of all became extinct.

A more horrible instance of woman-slaughter appears to have escaped unpunished, at least for a time. The Moonshee, Bunda Alee, in company with his wife, an infant daughter, and six servants, was taking to her bridegroom another daughter who had attained to a connubial age. On the journey he fell in with a numerous gang of Thugs, the leaders of whom contrived to ingratiate themselves with the Moonshee's party, and all travelled on together. One evening towards dusk some of the Thugs seated themselves, as usual, with the Moonshee at his tent door, and began to sing and play on the sitar. One of them presently took up the Moonshee's sword, which was lying on the ground at his feet, as if to examine it. The signal was then suddenly given, but the Moonshee sprung to his feet, screamed aloud, and tried to rush into the tent, but was instantly seized and strangled. His wife, hearing his shrieks, came running out with the infant in her arms, and shared his fate.

The bride was put to death within the tent. The servants were at that moment engaged in grooming the horses, and one of them crept under a horse's belly and lustily bawled out "murder!" but they were all quickly silenced by the fatal noose. Ghubboo Khan, who had murdered the mother, intended to adopt the infant, but was dissuaded by one of his comrades who pointed out that it might lead to their discovery. He therefore threw the child alive into the hole in which the dead bodies were already deposited, and the earth was hastily shovelled in upon the living and the dead. While this dreadful scene was enacting, a number of Khulasies were, within sight, occupied in pitching the tents of the European officers commanding a detachment of troops marching along the road. The Thugs, however, had taken care to play and sing, at the top of their voice, as soon as the butchery commenced, while others let loose two vicious horses and chased them with vociferous shouting, so as effectually to drown the cries of their victims.

The five years assigned as the duration of feminicide was simply a euphuism; it prevailed through a very much longer period. In 1816 a party of eighteen men and seven women were strangled near Shikarpore, but the Thugs spared two boys, one of whom, however, cried so bitterly and made so much moaning, that a ruffian seized him by the legs, swung him round, and dashed out his brains against a stone. The dead body was carelessly left lying on the ground, till a fisherman, passing that way, happened to see it, and went and reported the circumstance to the Thakoor Burjore Sing, of Powae. Guided by this clue, the Thakoor discovered the bodies of all the victims, and, collecting as many men as possible, gave chase to the murderers. Following their fresh traces he came up with them while washing themselves in a stream near the village of Tigura. Forming into a compact body, the Thugs retired upon the village, being repeatedly charged by the Thakoor's party, who ran one of them through the chest with a spear and sabred another. The villagers, however, expecting a share of the booty, turned out to the rescue of the Thugs and repulsed their assailants. Next morning they escorted them to the neighbouring village of Simareea, where they received the like sympathy and protection. This was no extraordinary occurrence, for the natives generally regarded the Thugs as a fraternity especially favoured by heaven. They would as soon have thought of destroying a snake or a wolf, or of opposing in any other way the decrees of Providence. The police, to save themselves trouble, and partly also from a secret dread of these mysterious and ruthless beings, used to declare that the dead bodies occasionally found in ravines, wells, and dry watercourses had been killed by tigers, and would burn them in all haste lest the marks of strangulation should be detected by their superiors. In the Deccan the task of suppression was rendered doubly difficult by the sullen opposition of the native chiefs, who sometimes even ventured to maltreat the police officers of the British Government. The Zemindars, or landowners, were always ready to give any amount of security for Thugs, against whom there was no sufficient evidence to justify their punishment. "They knew us very well," said an approver, "but they had then confidence in us; they thought we should keep our own secrets, and, if we did so, no one else would be able to convict us, and get them into trouble. Yes, there was then something like religion and good faith among us, and we found friends everywhere. Where could we find them now?" The Zemindars eagerly afforded them protection, because of the enormous rent they were wont to pay for their lands and villages. Valuable presents, also, were frequently made to them, at the same time that the Thugs engaged not to compromise their patrons by committing murder too near home. The Khyrooa chief once stood a siege from his lord, the Rajah of Jhansee, before he would surrender some eight or ten villains who had thrown themselves on his protection. And the Maharajah of Gwalior was obliged to send two guns and a small army against the Zemindar, or "laird," of Bahmanpora, to make him give up some Thugs whom he patronised; the firing lasted for some hours, and several lives were lost on both sides. Even those who affected to punish the miscreants, seldom touched their persons except to extort from them their ill-got treasures. They would seize one or two of the youngest, tie them up, and flog them till they confessed, or until the gang, in pity for their sufferings, pledged themselves to make up a certain sum, leaving two or three of their number as hostages. They were then released, and allowed to pursue their profession as before.

In the year 1812, soon after the murder of Lieutenant Monsell, a number of Thugs were arrested by certain Zemindars and grievously beaten, in the hope of making them bid high for their release. Their excessive cupidity, however, defeated its own ends. During their thirteen months imprisonment, forty of the Thugs perished from the dampness of their dungeon, combined with the ill-treatment they endured. The survivors insisted that their comrades were tortured to death by a demon, who entered the prison every night during the wet season. "I saw him," said one of them, "only once myself. I was awake while all the rest were asleep; he came in at the door, and seemed to swell as he came in till his head touched the roof, and the roof was very high, and his bulk became enormous. I prostrated myself, and told him that 'he was our Purmesur (great God), and we poor helpless mortals depending entirely upon his will.' This pleased him, and he passed by me; but took such a grasp at the man Mungulee, who slept by my side, that he was seized with spasms all over, from the nape of the neck to the sole of his foot." Of the Zemindars, who caused this atrocious suffering, he added, "not a soul of their families is now left to pour the libation at their funeral obsequies." How like is this to the glorious old Grecian idea of the avenging Nemesis! In truth, this was the only sort of justice administered in India during the supremacy of its native rulers—the golden age, according to the gentlemen of the Manchester school.

The Thugs made use of a peculiar dialect, called Ramasee, which was understood by the members of the fraternity throughout Hindostan, at Mooltan as at Arcot. The signification of the word Thug itself is "a deceiver;" they were likewise called Phanseegars, from the Hindostanee word Phansee, "a handkerchief." One Thug could always recognise another by his salutation *Aulae Khan, Salām*, if addressed to a Mussulmaun; or *Aulae Bhae, Ram, Ram*, if addressed to a Hindoo, equivalent to "Peace be with thee, friend!" A few specimens of their phraseology, selected from Captain Sleeman's Thug vocabulary, may be not altogether devoid of interest.

Aulae, or *Bora*, signified a Thug; *Beetoo*, or *Kuj*, everybody not a Thug; *Bagh*, *Phool*, a rendezvous; Boj' ha, the Thug who carried the bodies to the grave; *Bhukote*, or *Bhurtote*, the strangler; *Beyl*, site for murder; *Bykureea*, the scout of river Thugs; Beyl' ha, one who chose the place of murder; *Bunij*, literally merchandize—technically a traveller; *Bunij Ladhna*, "to load goods," *i.e.*, to murder; *Bhara* and *Ghurt ha*, dead bodies of victims; *Bisul purna*, to be awkwardly handled—to have the *roomal* caught on the face or head, instead of being slipped round the neck—the contrary of *soosul purna*: a Thug who was frequently guilty of bungling in this manner, was deposed from the honourable post of strangler; *Chookadena*, or *Thibaedena*, to get travellers to sit down and look up, by pointing out some star or object in the air, so that, the chin being raised, the handkerchief might be more easily passed round the throat; *Chumoseea*, or *Shumsheea*, the Thug whose duty it was to sieze the victim's hands; *Chumeea*, the Thug who held down the struggling victim; *Chandoo*, an expert Thug; *Cheesa*, a blessing from heaven, a rich traveller; *Dhonkee*, or *Ronkee*, a policeman or guard; *Dul*, weight; *Duller*, the head; *Doonr*, the shrieks of a victim; *Jywaloo*, left for dead, but afterwards recovering, which occasionally happened when there was not time to bury the bodies, or when it was judged imprudent to stab and slash them after being strangled; *Kuboola*, a tyro—the opposite of *Borka*—an adept. The latter could always gather together a band, for he was acquainted with the rites of initiation and the signification of omens, of which a *Kuboola* was generally quite ignorant. It was, consequently, found unnecessary to sentence the latter to perpetual imprisonment, as they could do little harm without the guidance of a *Borka*. A *Kuboola*, of the old Sindouse stock, once attempted to form a gang, into which he admitted all sorts of vagabonds, weavers, braziers, bracelet-makers, &c., who killed men and women indiscriminately, and neglected the most ordinary precautions. The natural consequence was, that they were soon detected, seized, and punished. On the other hand, one of the most noted Thugs on record was Sheikh Ahmed, of Arcot, whose gang consisted of sixty *Borkas*, disguised as recruits. This able leader had picked up the English words of command, with some knowledge of the Company's drill, and could even express himself intelligibly in English. He never displayed his wealth, which was considerable, or travelled in an ostentatious manner. On the contrary, when sixty years old and able to command the services of a hundred men, he would wander about for months with his wife, cooking his own food, going on foot, and living like a very poor man. His riches were concealed in various *caches*, regardless of the Horatian maxim, that silver shines only with reflected light from a temperate and judicious use. However, he escaped apprehension, and added, every year, with impunity, to his long catalogue of crime. But to return to the vocabulary—*Koojaoo*, an informer, or one who extorted hush-money from Thugs; *Khullee*, a Thug who, from ignoble care-giving impecuniosity, concealed himself on his return home to avoid his creditors—for the natives of Hindostan enjoy many of the blessings of an ancient and refined civilization; *Khomusna*, to rush in upon travellers when there was not sufficient time for the ordinary preparations; *Kanthuna*, or *Kanth dalna*, to stab when no opportunity was afforded for strangling—a very exceptional case—or to slash the suffocated victim, either to prevent revival, or the swelling of the body when buried, owing to the evolved gases finding no vent for escape. This gaseous inflation of the corpse was apt to cause the imposed earth to crack and open, when the horrid effluvia attracted jackals to the spot, who, by digging up the bodies, might discover the fact of a murder having been committed, and so lead to the detection of the murderers; *Kathee kurna*, to inveigle travellers, or to consult secretly as to the mode of doing away with them; *Kharoo*, a gang of Thugs; *Khuruk*, the sound of the consecrated pick-axe in making a grave, supposed to be audible only to the initiated; *Kurwa*, a square, or oblong grave, for one corpse or for many; *Gobba*, a circular grave, with a small pillar of earth left in the middle—it was believed to crack less than the ordinary grave, and was therefore preferred when the dead bodies were very numerous; *Kuthowa*, the Thug whose office it was to cut and stab the dead bodies; *Lugha*, the grave-digger; *Lutkuneea*, a very small purse, used exclusively by Thugs and professional thieves; *Maulee*, or *Phoola*, the Thug entrusted with the duty of taking to the village the money sent by the absent gang for the maintenance of their wives and families; *Nawureea*, a novice on his first expedition—sometimes they were compelled to kick the first murdered man five times on the back; *Nissar*, safe, as applied to any suitable place for lodging at, murdering, or dividing spoil—opposed to *tikkur*, unsafe; *Paoo*, an accomplice of Thugs; *Pehloo*, or *Sikka*, or *Roomal*, the handkerchief. This was, rather, a turban unfolded, or the long narrow cloth, or sash, worn round the waist. It was doubled to the length of about thirty inches, with a knot formed at the doubled extremity, and about eighteen inches from that a slip knot. The distance between these two knots was regulated by preparing the fatal instrument on the knee, which was made to do temporary duty for a neck. The use of the two knots was to give a firm hold. When the victim was fairly prostrated, the strangler adroitly loosened the slip knot, and made another fold of the cloth round his throat. Then placing his foot upon the back of his victim's neck, he drew the cloth tightly, as if—to use the informant's own words—he were "packing a bundle of straw." *Pehloo dena*, to instal as a strangler, of which more hereafter; *Phank*, a useless thing, a traveller without property; *Pungoo*, or *Bungoo*, a river Thug of Bengal, who murdered on board his *kuntee* or boat; *Phur*, same as *Beyl*, also a spot for dividing the plunder; *Phurjhana*, to clean the murder-spot—after a nocturnal murder, some of the gang were generally left behind to remove any signs of the crime that might be visible by daylight; *Phuruck dena*, to wave a cloth as signal of danger; *Pusur*, the direction of an expedition; *Ruhna*, a temporary grave; *Soon*, a Thug by birth, but not yet initiated; *Saur*, one who escaped from Thugs; *Sotha*, the inveigler; *Tome*, an article of extraordinary value; *Tilha*, a spy; *Thap*, a night encampment; *Tuppul*, a bye-path into which they often inveigled their unsuspecting travelling companions, as more convenient for their purposes. A rich traveller was called "a delicacy;" a poor one "a stick;" an old man "a barber's drum." Some of their signals, too, were quaint. The necessity of caution was inculcated by drawing the back of the hand along the chin, from the throat outwards; the open hand placed over the mouth and drawn gently downwards, implied the absence of danger. "Sweep the place," signified to look out; "bring firewood," take your places—that is, the place assigned to each Thug preparatory to action; "take out the handkerchief with the beetel," get the *roomal* ready, as already described; "eat beetel," or "hand the beetel," despatch him—this was called the *Jhirnee,* or signal to fall on; "look after the straw," get the body ready for burial; "the straw is come out," jackals have dug up the body. Another form of the *Jhirnee* was *Ae ho to ghyree chulo,* "if you are come, pray descend." When the scouts wished to report that all was safe, they called out as if to a comrade, "Bajeed Khan," or "Deo," or "Deoseyn." If the scouts saw any danger at hand, or a traveller coming along, they would call out "Sheikh Jee," or "Sheikh Mahommed," if they were Mussulmauns; and

"Luchmun Sing," or "Luchee Ram," or "Gunga Ram," if they were Hindoos. Sometimes the advanced guard of a gang, with victims in their power, would meet with a party of travellers, of whom they considered their friends in the rear were capable of disposing. In which case they sent some one back to tell Bajeed Khan, or Deoseyn, to make haste and overtake them. The others receiving this message understood that the coast was clear in front, and on meeting the travellers, lost no time in putting them to death. If a gang happened from any cause to get separated, they rallied with the cry, *Bukh*, *Bukh*, *Bukh*, "come, come, come." When the leader judged that the time was at hand for selecting a *beyl*, or site for murder, he would say to the Thug on whom that duty devolved, *Jao, kutoree manj lao*, "go and clean the brass cup." When he desired every one to repair to his post, he gave the *khokee*, that is, he made a great noise of hawking up phlegm from his throat; if anything then occurred to cause the suspension of operations, he gave the *thokee*, or spit out the phlegm. Otherwise, he exclaimed aloud "Surbulund Khan," or "Dulur Khan," or "Surmust Khan," whereupon the stranglers made ready and only awaited the *jhirnee*. Then the fatal words were pronounced, *Tombako kha lo*, or *pee lo*, "eat," or "drink (*i.e.*, smoke) your tobacco" —or one of the other formulæ was used—and the next instant the *roomal* was round the throat of the ill-fated wretch.

In order to avoid the suspicions likely to be engendered by very large bands of men travelling together, the Thugs used to break up into small parties of from three or four to a dozen or so, communicating with one another by a series of telegraphic signs, which enabled them to concentrate at any given point with amazing celerity. Thus, on coming to cross-roads, the leading files drew their feet along the dust in the direction they had taken. If they wished their comrades to follow quickly, they piled up some dust along the toe-line of their footmarks, on which they sometimes impressed their heel. Where there was no dust easily procurable, they left two stones, one upon the other, or strewed a few leaves to indicate the right path: if haste was needful, they would dispose the leaves in a long line.

Great as was the veneration entertained for the *roomal*, still greater was that accorded to the *kussee*, or pick-axe. It was consecrated with peculiar rites. On a day pronounced by the Pundit to be propitious, the leader betook him to a blacksmith—of course a member of his own fraternity—and closing the door, constrained him to relinquish all other work until the axe had been duly fabricated. One of the four auspicious days, Monday, Tuesday, Wednesday, or Friday, was then selected for the *dhoop*, or offering of incense, which took place within a house or tent, the shadow of no living thing being allowed to fall upon the axe. A Thug, renowned for his ceremonial lore, being appointed to officiate, the consecration was attempted—attempted, for it did not always succeed at the first trial. The officiating minister having taken his seat facing the west, received from the leader the pick-axe on a lordly brazen dish. A pit was then dug, over which the axe was held, and washed with water, and afterwards in succession with a mixture of sugar and water, sour milk, and ardent spirits, care being taken that the various liquids should flow into the pit. The next proceeding was to mark the axe from head to point with seven spots of red lead, and again place it on the brazen dish, together with a cocoa-nut, some cloves, paun leaves, gogul gum, inderjon, sessamum seeds, white sandal wood, and sugar. Ghee, or clarified butter, was also put into a small brass cup, standing by the side of the dish. A fire being now kindled with dried cow-dung and mango, or byr-wood, all these articles were thrown into it, excepting the cocoa-nut. So soon as the flames blazed high and bright, the priest, holding the axe in both hands, passed it through them seven times. Then, stripping off the rough outer coat of the cocoa-nut, he placed the fruit on the ground, and taking up the axe by the point, asked of the assembled Thugs, "Shall I strike?" All having replied in the affirmative, he struck the nut with the butt-end of the axe, and usually shivered it into fragments. The whole of the shell and some of the kernel being thrown into the fire, the axe was wrapt in a clean white cloth and laid on the ground, pointing to the west, the Thugs facing the same quarter of the heavens and worshipping. This act of adoration done, they all partook of the cocoa-nut, and collecting the fragments, threw them into the pit. Should the Thibaoo now be heard, all was duly performed, and the axe was a holy thing—no longer a *kodalee*, but a *kussee*. But if the Pilhaoo first smote upon their ears, or the priest failed to crack the nut at a blow, the ceremonies must be repeated—all had been done in vain.

On the march, the sacred *kussee* was always intrusted to a Thug of approved sobriety and steadiness, who carried it in his waist-belt. While encamped it was buried in a secure place, with the point turned towards the direction intended to be pursued. If a better road could be taken, the axe would be found pointing that way. No human foot was allowed to tread the ground beneath which it reposed; nor should the touch of any unclean man or thing ever pollute its purity. If a well happened to be near, it was thrown into it, instead of being buried; and when the gang was ready to set out, being duly summoned, it came of its own accord to its bearer. Nay, more, if a dozen *kussees* were thrown into the same well, each would fly unerringly to its proper guardian. When this startling assertion was made, Captain Sleeman suggested it was a clever piece of jugglery; whereupon an approver indignantly exclaimed: "What! shall not a hundred generations of Thugs be able to distinguish the tricks of man from the miracles of God? Is there not the difference of heaven and earth between them! Is not one a mere trick, and the other a miracle, witnessed by hundreds assembled at the same time?" Another approver capped his rhetorical friend, by declaring that he had seen with his own eyes this miracle performed in favour of the Arcottee Thugs, as the reward of their superior piety and strict observance of omens.

The burnt-offerings were repeated on all holy days, and after any unusual interval between murders. After being used, it was washed with solemn rites. There was no more binding oath than to swear by the *kussee*. If the axe itself were not procurable, it sufficed to make an effigy of it in cloth or clay. The person attested, held it in his hand as he swore, and then drank the water in which it had been previously bathed, A perjurer died an awful death within six days after his guilt, his head gradually turning round till his face stood over his back. After all, this is not more strange than the old Hebrew trial of jealousy, as described in the fifth chapter of the Book of Numbers; nor more ridiculous than any ordeal in which supernatural effects were expected from simple and natural causes. If the *kussee* fell from the hand of its bearer, his death was certain to ensue within twelve months, or else some dire calamity befel the gang. The immediate results of the untoward accident were his deposition from his high office, a change of route, and a fresh consecration of the axe. It has been before remarked, that no one but a Thug could hear the sound of the *kussee*, when used in digging graves. It had likewise another virtue, in common with the *roomal*. "Are you never afraid," asked Captain Sleeman, one day, of some of the approvers, "of the spirits of the persons you murder?"

"Never," they replied, "they cannot trouble us."

"Why? Do they not trouble other men when they commit murder?"

"Of course they do. The man who commits a murder is always haunted by spirits. He has sometimes fifty at a time upon him, and they drive him mad."

"And how do they not trouble you?"

"Are not the people we kill, killed by the orders of Davey? Do not all whom we kill, go to Paradise, and why should their spirits stay to trouble us? . . . . . A good deal of our security from spirits is to be attributed to the *roomal*, with which we strangle."

"I did not know that there was any virtue in the *roomal*."

"Is it not our *sikka* (ensign), as the pick-axe is our *nishan* (standard)? . . . . More is attributable to the pick-axe. Do we not worship it every seventh day? Is it not our standard? Is its sound ever heard when digging the grave of any but a Thug? And can any man ever swear to a falsehood upon it?"

Next to the leader of the gang, the most important personages were the stranglers. Before a Thug could hope to attain this honourable distinction, he must have served on several expeditions, and given proof of courage and impassibility. The usual gradations were, employment as a scout, then as a grave-digger, afterwards as a holder of hands, and finally he might become a strangler. So soon as his mind was inflamed with this ambition, he had recourse to one of the oldest and most famous of the brotherhood, and besought him to act as *gooroo*, or spiritual preceptor, and to accept him as his *cheyla*, or disciple. If his request were granted, the *gooroo* led him into a field, with three or four experienced Thugs, and all placed themselves facing the direction in which the gang was about to move. Then the *gooroo* lifted up his voice, and prayed aloud:—"O Kalee, Kunkalee, Bhudkalee! O Kalee, Mahakalee, Calcutta Walee! if it seemeth to thee fit that the traveller now at our lodging should die by the hands of this thy slave, vouchsafe us the Thibaoo." Should the auspicious omen be refused, the candidate must wait until another opportunity. But if the goddess smiled upon his vows, the party returned to their quarters, and the *gooroo*, taking a handkerchief, and looking towards the west, tied a knot in one end of it, inserting therein a rupee or other silver coin. This knot was called *goor ghaut*, or the classic knot, and was a very artistic performance, the end of the *roomal* being skilfully folded inwards. The disciple thereupon respectfully took the handkerchief in his right hand, and went and stood over his sleeping victim—for a feeble person, and one asleep, was generally chosen for the maiden trial of skill. When all was ready, the *Shumsheea*, or hand-holder, suddenly awakened the sleeper with the cry that a snake or a scorpion was under or beside him. As he started up, bewildered with sleep and terror, the *roomal* was slipped over his neck, and in a few seconds he had ceased to fear either reptiles or baser men. The deed being satisfactorily accomplished, the *cheyla* bowed lowly before his preceptor, and touched his feet with both hands, a compliment he also paid to all the *gooroo's* relatives and friends there present. After the Thibaoo had again been heard, he untied the knot, and presented the coin, with whatever silver he possessed, to his teacher, who added to it whatever money he happened to have upon his own person. Of this amount half a crown was expended in the purchase of *goor*, or coarse sugar, and the rest in sweetmeats. The Tapoonee feast was then held under a neem, mango, or byr-tree, the *cheyla* sitting with the Bhurtotes, or stranglers, and receiving a like share of the consecrated *goor*. At the conclusion of the expedition, the tyro entertained his preceptor's family, and gave to him and his wife a present of new clothes. The entertainment was returned by the *gooroo*, between whom and his pupil an indissoluble connection existed ever afterwards unto death.

The Tapoonee, to which allusion has just been made, was a sacrifice offered to Bhowanee after every murder. A half-crown's worth of coarse sugar having been procured through the instrumentality of one of their most plausible members —for the purchase of so large a quantity at a time might have excited strange surmises—it was placed on a blanket, or sheet, spread upon a clear spot of ground. The *kussee*, or sacred pickaxe, and a silver coin—by way of *roop dursun*, or silver offering—were also laid upon the sheet, beside the pile of sugar. The most experienced of the leaders there present then seated himself on the edge of the sheet, facing to the west, and on either side of him were ranged as many

Bhurtotes as could be accommodated on the carpet, but taking care that they should make an even number. The others sat behind these. The leader next made a hole in the ground, and dropping into it a pinch of the *goor*, raised his eyes to the sky, and, with clasped hands, devoutly prayed aloud:—"Great goddess! as thou didst vouchsafe one lakh and 62,000 rupees (£16,200) to Jora Naick and Koduk Bunwaree in their need, so, we pray thee, fulfil our desires!" These words were repeated by the entire assembly; after which the leader sprinkled a little water over the pit and the *kussee*, and placed some *goor* on the hand of every Thug seated on the blanket. Some one then uttered the *jhirnee*, or signal for strangulation, and the *goor* was eaten in solemn silence. Not a word was spoken until the whole of the consecrated pile had disappeared, and been washed down with a draught of pure water. If any crumbs fell on the ground they were carefully picked up and thrown into the hole; for should any beast of the field, or bird of the air, partake of the holy offering, the wrath of the goddess would burn for years. The silver coin being restored to its owner, the unconsumed sugar was distributed among the lower and junior grades of the association. But if any one of the uninitiated, by chance or design, tasted of that to which the stranglers only were entitled, he was straightway irresistibly impelled to Thuggee, and never could the charm that bound him be broken or counteracted.

When necessity, or the weariness of inactivity, or the fascination of their terrible calling, urged them to leave their tranquil homes, their wives and families; the leader of the gang, accompanied by four of his ablest followers, would seat themselves on a blanket around a long-experienced and venerable sage; while the vulgar herd sat down surrounding this group at a little distance. In front of the pundit was placed a brass plate containing a few grains of wheat and rice, and two copper coins. The leader having respectfully inquired on what day they should set out, and in what direction, the pundit went through various ceremonies, too trivial to be particularized, and then indicated the day, the hour, and the route. When the appointed period had arrived—it could not be a Wednesday, or a Thursday, or in the months of July, September, or December—the leader filled a *lotah*, or brass vessel, with water, and carried it with his right hand over its mouth and holding it by his side. Some turmeric, two copper coins and one of silver, together with the head of the pickaxe, were next tied up separately in a clean white handkerchief, which the leader pressed against his breast in his left hand. Then turning to the heaven-selected direction he slowly moved with all the gang to a field outside the village, where finding a suitable spot, and still preserving the same attitude, he paused, and in seeming abstraction, prayed: "Great goddess! Universal Mother! If this our meditated expedition be good in thy sight, vouchsafe unto us help, and the signs of thy approbation!" The other Thugs repeated his words, and praised their patron, Bhowanee. Within half an hour afterwards the Pilhaoo ought to be heard on the left and the Thibaoo on the right hand. Then, and not till then, the leader relaxed from his statue-like attitude, and putting the *lotah* on the ground, himself sat down, still looking in the same direction. Thus he remained seven hours communing with himself, his abstraction being finally interrupted by his followers bringing him food and informing him that all things were ready. The silver and copper coins and the turmeric he carefully preserved throughout the expedition, and on his return presented them to some poor Brahman, unless great good fortune had attended his party, in which case they were kept for the opening of the next expedition. If the *lotah* had fallen from his hand before the omens were given, he would assuredly have died within twelve, or at the latest, within twenty-four months. The preparations being completed, the gang struck off in the direction indicated by the pundit; but after taking a few steps they could turn aside as circumstances might seem to recommend.

During the first seven days after their departure the females of their respective families held no intercourse with those belonging to another gang, lest the victims intended for their own friends should fall into the power of the others. The Thugs, themselves, for the like period abstained from animal food, and even from their favourite *ghee,* and partook of no other food than fish, *goor,* and *dal* (a kind of pulse). Nor did they shave or allow their clothes to be washed, or indulge in alms'-giving—which, with personal abstinence, constitutes the Hindoo notion of practical religion. On the seventh day they had a grand feast, in which green vegetables of some kind made a prominent figure. If a victim, however, were obtained within these seven days of probation, all restraints were at once cancelled and abandoned. Should the expedition last no longer than one year, they frequently denied themselves the taste of milk throughout, and likewise refrained from brushing their teeth. Any bad omens encountered prior to the second halt sufficed to break off the expedition; after that point they could be averted by expiatory rites. It was considered unfortunate to hear any one lamenting the dead as they started, or to meet an inhabitant of their own village, or an oil-vender, carpenter, potter, dancing-master, a maimed or lame person, a fakir (Mussulmaun religious mendicant) with a brown waist-band, or a jogee (Hindoo religious mendicant) with long interwoven hair. But it promised well to fall in with a fair in any other village than their own, or a corpse, or to see a party of female friends weeping round a bride as she left her parents' house to go to her husband's.

As a general rule, the different divisions of a gang used to encamp near each other at the various halting grounds, and were always in frequent communication with one another. No sooner had one of them fallen in with a party of travellers than the intelligence was conveyed to all the others, and every one was on the alert. Their leaders, travelling as merchants, gentlemen, soldiers, or peasants, usually succeeded by their plausible manners in ingratiating themselves with the strangers. And there was nothing formidable or repulsive in their outward appearance. On the contrary, they are described as being mild and benevolent of aspect, and peculiarly courteous, gentle, and obliging. Unlike most of the natives of India, they travelled unarmed, with the exception of two or three who carried daggers. It was therefore an apparently reasonable request on their part to be allowed to proceed under the protection of those who made a grand display of their swords and spears and fire-arms.

This request being usually accorded, the united parties journeyed on together, chatting and prattling with the volubility and easy familiarity of orientals. Sometimes days would elapse before a favourable opportunity occurred. There is an instance mentioned of a gang having accompanied a family of eleven persons for twenty days, during which they had traversed upwards of 200 miles, and then murdered the whole of them, though the head of the family had only one arm, and ought therefore to have been spared. Another gang accomplished 160 miles in twelve days, in company with a party of sixty—men, women and a child—before they found an eligible occasion.

They preferred committing murder in the evening, when the travellers would be seated on the ground, mingled with themselves, talking, smoking, singing, and playing the sitar. Where it could be done without suspicion, three Thugs were allotted to every victim. So soon as the fatal signal was given, one seized hold of his hands, the second grasped his legs and held him down, while the strangler tightened the *roomal* round his neck, and only relaxed the strain when life was extinct. Then the bearers of the daggers slashed the dead bodies, the grave-diggers quickly excavated a deep trench, the corpses were stripped and thrown in, the earth was hastily shovelled in and trampled down, and in an incredibly short space of time all traces were completely effaced of the terrible tragedy. When the ground was too hard to admit of a grave being dug, or any other cause intervened to prevent the burial, the bodies were flung into a ravine, or well, or water course, or concealed in the jungle. Not unfrequently it happened that no convenient opportunity was presented for murdering the travellers while seated. In this case, an experienced Thug would be sent forward to select a *beyl*, or suitable spot, on arriving at which, if the scouts reported a clear coast, the gang would close upon their unsuspecting companions and speedily put them to death. It was more difficult when the travellers were mounted, though the fleetest charger could not avail to save his rider. A horseman was always attacked by three men; one walked at his horse's head, a second a little way in the rear, and a third by his side, pleasantly conversing with him until the signal was given, when he suddenly dragged him out of the saddle and, with the assistance of his comrade, strangled him before he could recover his self-possession. It was thought a subject for just pride when a Thug pulled a traveller from his horse and murdered him without aid. Such an exploit was a patent of nobility, and conferred credit upon the third and fourth generation. The Thugs, even as approvers, used to glory in the recollection of their past achievements, and spoke of them with as much animation as a sportsman exhibits in describing a good day's shooting or a capital run with the hounds. To avoid confusion, they would distinguish the grand murders by the number of victims they had killed. Thus, in the chaleesrooh, or forty-soul affair, thirty-one men, seven women and two girls were murdered by a collective force of 360 Thugs, who divided among themselves £1,700 worth of plunder. A few days previously 160 of this gang had disposed of a party consisting of a widow, a slave-girl and twelve armed followers. The Sartrooh, or sixty-soul affair, is an excellent illustration of their ordinary mode of operations. The Thugs travelled with this numerous party, consisting of fifty-two men, seven women, and a Brahman boy, about four years old, for twenty days before they consummated their purpose. At Sehora they persuaded their companions to quit the high road and take one that led through the jungles. However, they patiently went on with them, gaining more and more upon their confidence, till they had come to Chittakote. "There," said one of them to Captain Sleeman, "we sent on people as usual to select a place for the murder, and they found one about five miles distant, in a very extensive jungle, without a human habitation for many miles on either side. We persuaded the party to set out soon after midnight; and as they went along, we managed to take our appointed places, two Thugs by every traveller, and the rest in parties of reserve at different intervals along the line, every two managing to keep the person they were appointed to kill, in conversation. On reaching the place chosen, the signal was given at several different places, beginning with the rear party, and passing on to that in front; and all were seized and strangled except the boy. It was now near morning, and too late to admit of the bodies being securely buried; we made a temporary grave for them in the bed of the river, covered them over with sand, and went on with the boy and the booty to Chittakote, intending to send back a large party the next night and have the bodies securely buried. The rains had begun to set in, and after the murders it rained very heavily all the day. The party, however, went back, but found that the river had risen and washed away all the bodies, except two or three, which they found exposed, and pushed into the stream to follow the rest."

So recently as 1830 Bhowanee was believed to have saved her votaries the trouble of burying their victims. A gang after wandering about Loodhiana, Sirhind, and Umballah, came to Goolchutter, where they performed their ablutions in the sacred tank and rested three days. "Having then proceeded two miles towards Kurnal, they overtook two travellers from Mooltan on their way to Muttra, mounted on ponies. They were in appearance very poor." So poor, indeed, that it was judged they would not pay for the trouble of killing them, and they had nearly escaped until a speculative Thug offered to give £10 for whatever might be found upon them. "Their death was accordingly determined on, and they were conducted by the Thugs to Turowlee where they rested in the Serai ('accommodation for man and beast'), and Cheyne Jemadar invited the poor wretches to partake of a repast." The travellers, being religious mendicants, had many anecdotes to tell of their adventures and travels, and pleasantly beguiled the early hours of darkness. Next morning they all set out together and had not gone very far before the *jhirnee* was given, and the mendicants ceased to beg and to breathe. But while their grave was being dug, the neighing of horses was heard coming along the road, which caused the Thugs to flee to a place of concealment, leaving the corpses on the ground. The horsemen passed on, and saw or suspected nothing. Then the Thugs came out from their hiding places, but lo! the bodies had disappeared—but not so their property which amounted to the value of several hundred pounds. It is true religious mendicants were exempted from strangulation, but this was clearly an exceptional case, for Bhowanee had positively commanded their death by sending favourable omens; she had, besides, rewarded her worshippers with a rich booty, and even disposed of the dead bodies, whose souls had gone straight to Paradise.

They were not, however, always equally fortunate. A gang once learnt from the spies that four travellers with property were trudging along the road towards Baroda. Instantly, twenty fine stout fellows set out after them, and after a long chase came up with the travellers and murdered them. "To the great disappointment and chagrin of us all," bewailed one of the gang, "no property was found upon them, for they turned out to be common stone-cutters, and their tools tied in bundles, which they carried over their shoulders, deceived the spies into the supposition that they were carrying treasure." At another time a gang fell in with two Ganges-water carriers, two tailors, and a woman, and next day they were joined by two very poor travellers, of whom they tried in vain to disembarrass themselves. They would start at night without awakening them, but somehow the others *would* hear their preparations and insist upon accompanying them. The Thugs then appointed four of their brethren to detach these unconscious suicides from the rest of the party and keep them on the high road while the others struck off down a byepath. This device also failed, for they became frightened and could be satisfied with nothing less than a junction with the main body. Their obstinacy sealed their fate. Half a dozen of the Thugs went on with them in advance, and strangling them, found upon them only one rupee—worth about two shillings. The others soon shared the fate of the two poor travellers, but turned out a more profitable prize, as they yielded among them twenty pounds. A smaller sum, however, than one shilling will often times tempt a Hindoo to commit murder, even though he have nothing to do with Thuggee. What value the latter attached to life may be inferred from the testimony of one of themselves. "I have never strangled any one," said he, "but have aided in throwing bodies into wells. Eight annas (one shilling) is a very good remuneration for murdering a man. We often strangle a victim who is suspected of having two pice (one farthing)." But it seldom happened that a murder produced less than two pounds; the average being probably about fifteen pounds. It is almost comical to read that these dread beings were sometimes robbed at night by vulgar pilferers, though they usually set a watch. The same sort of retribution is observable in the fate of twenty-seven Dacoits, or gang-robbers, who had in their possession at the time above £1,300 worth of money, gold ornaments, gems, and shawls. A gang of one hundred and twenty-five Thugs having met with them, begged to be allowed to travel under their protection. The Dacoits carelessly assented, and were shortly afterwards all put to death.

Eager as they were for booty the Thugs appear to have been courteous and forbearing towards one another, and equitable in the division of their spoils. Feringeea and twenty-six of his gang were one day cooking their dinners under some trees by the road-side when five travellers came bye, but could not be persuaded to stop and partake of their meal, saying they intended to sleep at Hirora that night, and they had yet eight miles to go. The Thugs followed after them, and also reached Hirora, but could discover no traces of the travellers. Feringeea, therefore, inferred that they must have fallen into the hands of another gang, and suddenly recollected having passed an encampment of Brinjarees (bullock-drivers) not far from the town. On the following morning he accordingly went back with a few of his comrades, and at once recognised a horse and a pony which he had observed in the possession of the travellers. "What have you done with the five travellers, my good friends?" he said. "You have taken from us our *merchandize.*" They apologised for what they had done, pleading ignorance, and offered to share the booty; but this Feringeea declined, saying that he had no claim to a share, as none of his party was present at the *loading.*

The division of the spoils was regulated with great nicety. The leaders were usually entitled to every tenth article, and to one anna in the rupee (one sixteenth) of actual money, besides their share as individuals. If the gang consisted of twenty, including the Jemadar, the booty was divided into twenty-one equal parts, of which the Jemadar received two. Five per cent. was then set aside for the stranglers, and the rest divided into three equal heaps, corresponding to as many equal sections of the gang. Each section marked a cowree (a shell), and the three were put into a man's hand without his knowing to which either belonged, who then placed one on each pile. The sections afterwards divided among themselves each its own lot.

A feast was sometimes held in honour of Davee, in the course of an expedition. If the expenses were defrayed by subscription, as was most customary, it was called a Punchaetee Kotee, and was usually celebrated during the

Hooley or Dusserah festivals. Occasionally a single member provided the feast; but, to be entitled to do so, he must have been a strangler, or at least a Thug in the third generation. The feast was in this wise. Having procured some goats, of whom two must be perfectly black, without speck or blemish, and a sufficient quantity of rice, *ghee*, spices, and spirits, they assembled in a room the doors and windows of which could be closed, so as to prevent any prying eyes from seeing what was passing within. The floor being carefully swept and plastered with cow-dung, a square space, measuring a cubit each way, was drawn in the middle of the apartment, with a mixture of turmeric and lime. On this square was spread a clean white sheet, whereon was placed some boiled rice, and on the top of that the half of a cocoa-nut shell filled with *ghee*, in which floated two cotton wicks lying across each other, so as to give four lights. If a cocoa-nut was not procurable, a vessel of the same form was shapened in dough. Upon the sheet were then laid the sacred pickaxe, the dagger of the gang (the *miséricorde*), and the spirits. The two black goats were next washed and thoroughly wetted, and placed with their faces to the westward. If one, or both of them shook off the wet with lusty vigour, it was a sign that the sacrifice was acceptable; otherwise, the rice and spirits alone were consumed, and without any further ceremony. But in the former case, if Mahommedans, they chaunted a sort of grace as they cut the throats of the whole of the animals; if Hindoos, they struck off their heads at a blow. The skins, bones, and offal were thrown into a pit dug for the purpose. When every man's appetite was satiated, they washed their face and hands over the pit, and filled it up and levelled it with the ground. Should any profane eye witness any part of the preparations, or a spark fall on the sheet and burn a hole, or any animal touch the offal, the leader must expect to die within a year and all his companions would come to grief.

Besides the land Thugs there was a bold and skilful clan calling themselves Bungoos, or Pungoos, who practised the same vocation on the Hooghly river, going up as far as Benares or even Cawnpore, but chiefly infesting the Burdwan district. Their system and dialect differed considerably from those of their land brethren. Their leaders assumed the appearance of the proprietor or captain of a passenger boat, while some of his gang bent to the oars or towed the vessel along the bank, and the others, dressed as pilgrims or shopkeepers, took their seat on deck; these were the stranglers and their assistants. A few of the most plausible and insinuating members were employed as *Sothas*, or inveiglers. These wandered on the roads leading to the various Ghauts, or landing places, and contrived to get into conversation with the travellers who seemed bound for the river. On arriving at the Ghaut they would see a clean tidy boat, already partially filled with passengers and ready to swing off. They naturally hastened on board, rejoicing at not being detained. The river Thugs always faced their victims, sitting in a row on one side of the deck opposite to them. So soon as an opportunity presented itself, the look-out man smote the deck three times with his hand. Then the helmsman gave the *jhirnee,* by exclaiming *Bhugna ko paun do,* "give my sister's son some paun." Up sprang the pretended voyagers, and throwing the *roomal* round the neck of their victims pressed it tightly in front, bending their head backwards, while their assistants held their feet and hands. Though sometimes one Thug would almost suffice for the purpose, nine of them have been known to strangle seven men stronger than themselves, and twelve have overpowered ten. When the convulsive writhings had ceased, they made certainty doubly sure by breaking the backbone and violently kicking or punching their victims with their elbows. The bodies were then pushed into the river through a window made in either side of the boat, immediately above the water-mark. The greatest care was taken to avoid shedding any blood, which by discolouring the stream might lead to suspicion and detection. If a drop were spilt, they returned home and offered up expiatory sacrifices. Women were invariably permitted to escape, and all property of a suspicious character was at once destroyed. Their proceedings, however, were no secret to the river police, whose silence was secured by rich presents. Their very existence was thus kept from the knowledge of the European magistrates until the year 1836, but in little more than twelve months afterwards 161 of the miscreants had been arrested, and the names obtained of thirty-eight others. There were usually about fourteen to each boat, and there were eighteen boats regularly occupied in this dreadful business, besides several engaged for occasional service. The hot and wet seasons were deemed equally unfavourable, as few travellers were then abroad; the most productive months being November,

December, January, and February. A party of river Thugs, occupying two boats, contrived to become acquainted with the *Manjee*, or commander of a boat laden with tobacco and hemp, and persuaded him and his crew to stop with them at a *chur*, or sand-bank, and cook their dinners together. After the repast the Thug leader asked the others to join his party in fulfilling a vow he had made to the god Hurry Sote. So they all sang the song of Hurry Sote, when the leader suddenly exclaimed, "Now, Hurry, give us our plunder!" Five Thugs instantly leaped on the throats of the Manjee and his crew, threw them back upon the sand and strangled them. Then their comrades fell upon the lifeless corpses, broke their backbones, punched them on the ribs with their fists and elbows, and dragging them into the deep running water let them float down the stream.

Perhaps a better idea than has yet been given of the nature and extent of Thuggee, may be derived from Captain Sleeman's Official Report of an Expedition into Malwa, Guzerat, Kandeish, and Berar, by gangs from Gwalior, Bundlecund, and the Saugor districts, in 1827-28. The leader was our old friend Feringeea, who started from Gorha with twenty-five Thugs and proceeded to Moghul ka Serai, where he fell in with two Mahrattas. These were put to death about three miles further on. Arriving at Tuppa, in Indore, the gang was then joined by eleven more Thugs, who all went on together to Raghooghur, where they met two Mahrattas and a Marwaree on their way from Saugor to Indore. Here Soper Sing and fifteen Thugs came up with them, escorting a bird-catcher and two shopkeepers journeying from Indore to Patna. All six were strangled in the night and buried in one grave. Next morning Feringeea's party, with five of Soper Sing's crossed the Nerbudda at the Puglana Ghaut, and at Samneer murdered three Sipahees, in search of service, at mid-day, and left their bodies by the road side. The next stage was Kurajgow Kuringee, whence they accompanied a traveller, who was going towards the south, for sixteen miles, where they killed him and buried his corpse beneath the walls of a small Hindoo temple. Thence they passed through Omrowtee to Larun Kurnajee, and in their camp in a grove killed a traveller whom they had brought on with them from Bam; and also a thief found skulking among some tombs, who had one hundred and ten pounds worth of stolen goods in his possession. At Busum their numbers were swelled by a reinforcement of fifty Thugs under four leaders. Going on together in one body they encamped near Nandair, and there murdered five travellers. Some of the new arrivals having again left them, the others held on to Rovegow, where they overtook nine persons, whom they accompanied about three miles and strangled just before daybreak. At Hyderabad they lodged near the bridge over the Hoosa Nuddee, where they killed and buried a Brahman and two Rajpoots with whom they had scraped an acquaintance in the Bhegan Bazar. Wandering on to Gungakhera they fell in with three Marwarees, whom they escorted a stage on the Holwa road. One of the travellers being accidentally thrown from his horse, was instantly strangled, and his companions of course shared the same fate. As they had not reached the appointed *Beyl,* they left the bodies upon the ground, a prey to jackals and carnivorous birds. Their next encampment was at Purureea, in Holwa, where they murdered a Soobahdar (native commissioned officer), five sepoys, and a woman. At Doregow they met three Pundits and with them a Byragee (Hindoo ascetic), mounted on a pony, plastered over with sugar and covered with flies. Driving away the mendicant, they killed and buried the Pundits. On leaving Doregow the Byragee again joined them and went on in their company to Raojana, where they overtook six cloth-merchants travelling from Bombay to Nagpore. As the mendicant was much in their way, they pelted him with stones, and having thus got rid of him they killed the merchants, burying their bodies in the grove. The next day the Byragee again joined them and proceeded with them to Mana, where they fell in with two bearers and a sepoy. Shaking off their troublesome companion, they hastened on to the spot selected for the contemplated murder, where the mendicant once more came up with them. Their patience being exhausted, they offered one of the gang ten shillings extra to kill him and take the sin upon himself. All four were then strangled, and, to their astonishment, the Byragee proved the most valuable prize of all; for upon him and his pony they found many pounds weight of coral, 350 strings of small pearls, fifteen strings of large pearls, and a gilded necklace. Soon after they arrived at Omrowtee, between which and Nadgow they got hold of two men, whom they murdered at their encampment. They were treasure bearers and had with them £400 worth of silver. These are a peculiar class of men, excessively poor, but famed for their honesty. They were never known to betray their trust, and would rather yield their life than surrender their charge. They bore no weapons, chiefly relying on the poverty of their garb and external appearance. The Bombay and Surat merchants used to employ them in conveying specie through Kandeish and Surat to Indore and Rajpootana, and they generally succeeded in escaping the notice of mere marauders; but it was a different thing with the Thugs who took life officially and professionally, content with a farthing but oftener reaping a fruitful harvest.

From Nadgow the band proceeded to Kuragow, and soon afterwards in passing through a small dry ravine fell in with four men driving two bullocks laden with copper pice. The men were instantly put to death, and their bodies slightly covered with stones and rubbish. After this affair two of their leaders with their respective followers returned home, while the others strolled onwards through Burhanpore to Indore, where they received an accession of strength by the junction of three leaders with sixty Thugs.

Three Marwarees being here inveigled into a house occupied by a part of the gang, never again went forth into the road. They remained at Indore a whole day, but were not idle, for Feringeea prevailed upon four more Marwarees to accompany him to the encampment of the remainder of the gang, and they likewise were dismissed to Hades. Soon after leaving Indore they fell in with four travellers, whom they murdered in camp that evening. Feringeea's party then diverged from the main body and passed through Saugor to Chutterpore, where intelligence was received that a body of armed men were in pursuit of them. They, therefore, doubled back and came to Kondee, a short distance from which they murdered two travellers. At Raghooghur they were reinforced by twelve of their fraternity, and on the following day by thirty more under Sheikh Inaent: and at Dubohee, near Bhilsa, they were joined by two more leaders with twenty Thugs. Here they murdered two sepoys. After this affair fifty of them under Sheik Inaent went on to Baroda, where they all fell sick and were glad to return to Bheelpore. Their convalescence was celebrated by the murder of two Bearers. Encouraged by this success they journeyed to Oodeypore in the Dhar Pergunnah. Three sepoys and another man were strangled next morning about two miles from the town. A little further on they overtook an elephant driver, in the service of the Oodeypore Rajah, and him they murdered at night at a village called Amjhera. Passing through Mhow, to a village on the side of Raghooghur, they fell in with three Bearers, whom they strangled next morning. They then held on through Ashta till they encountered a Havildar (non-commissioned native officer), a sepoy, and another, of whom they disposed the following morning. Shortly afterwards a large portion of this gang returned home, whereon the Sheikh went off and rejoined Feringeea. Their junction had scarcely been effected before it was announced that the police were close upon their track. Many more of the Thugs then started off homewards, and others retreated to a stream near Peepala, where, notwithstanding their fears, they made away with two sepoys, another man, and a woman.

A village called Jhundawala was the scene of their next exploit—a Bearer their next victim. After that they came to Tuppa, and, as they were setting out next morning, were joined by a Havildar, a sepoy, and two women, whom they murdered on the following day. Arriving at Kenjarra they strangled two more sepoys, and four more a few days afterwards. The gang then broke up, and Feringeea returned to his home in Tehree. Since he last parted from his wife, unconscious of his crimes, he had been an accomplice in the murder of one hundred men and five women. Let not this appalling number appear incredible. In the kingdom of Oude, a fair sample of native government, there were 1406 miles of road infested by Thugs, and no fewer than two hundred and seventy-four *Beyls*, or sites of murder; that is, one in every five miles and a half. Twenty Thugs, admitted as Approvers, acknowledged that they were present, respectively, at 508, 931, 350, 377, 604, 119, 42, 103, 264, 203, 195, 294, 117, 322, 340, 28, 65, 81, 153, and twenty-four murders, the least experienced having witnessed twenty-four murders, and the most 931—thus giving an average of 256 murders to each of the twenty. The same Beyl was not unfrequently the scene of several murders. Captain Sleeman mentions a striking instance of this. When Feringeea was first brought before him a prisoner, in December 1830, he offered, if his life were spared, to give information that would lead to the arrest of some large gangs who had appointed to rendezvous at Jyepore in the following February. Some incredulity as to his power to do so having been expressed, he begged to be allowed to accompany the "Sahib" a short distance on his official tour of inspection, when he would afford ample evidence as to his knowledge of Thuggee. He promised no more than he was able to perform. Two stages from Saugor on the road to Seronge, Captain Sleeman encamped for the night in a small mango grove near the village of Selohda. At an early hour of the next morning Feringeea desired to see him, and pointing to three different spots declared they were so many graves. "A Pundit and six attendants, murdered in 1818, lay among the ropes of my sleeping tent, a Havildar and four Sipahees murdered in 1824, lay under my horses, and four Brahman carriers of Ganges-water and a woman, murdered soon after the Pundit, lay within my sleeping-tent. The sward had grown over the whole, and not the slightest sign of its ever having been broken was to be seen." All night long Mrs. Sleeman had tossed about in her sleep, tormented by horrible dreams, probably engendered by the foul air arising from so many graves—certainly not caused by the spirits of the departed, and, perhaps, many a ghost story may owe its origin to some similar cause. Still doubting, Captain Sleeman sent for the police and a posse of villagers, who after digging down about five feet came upon the skeletons of the

Havildar and his comrades, and afterwards the others were discovered in succession. Feringeea then proposed to discover other graves in the neighbouring groves, but Captain Sleeman could stand no more of such horrors for that morning. It transpired that the Pundit's horse had been presented to the proprietor of the village, in which some of the gang actually resided, and that the others came thither every year and stopped some time "feasting, carousing and murdering," and yet neither the police nor the inhabitants appeared to have the slightest suspicion of the real nature of their pursuits. It must be remembered that they never murdered any but strangers and wayfarers, and that the villagers and their property would be perfectly secure. It would be an excess of charity, however, to suppose that the Zemindar had not a shrewd guess as to the means by which his horse was obtained. During the three years, 1822 to 1824, both inclusive, that Captain Sleeman was magistrate of the Nursingpore district in the Nerbuddah valley, and—as he imagined—cognizant of every crime and every bad character within its limits, he was perfectly unconscious that there was a Thug village only 400 yards from the Court-house, and that only a few miles distant the groves of Mundaisur contained fully one hundred dead bodies. These groves were a favourite place of rendezvous for gangs coming from Upper India and from the Deccan, with the connivance and under the protection of two respectable landholders, descendants of the pious individuals who had planted those trees to shelter the unhoused wanderer.

The destruction of life and property since the commencement even of the present century must have been enormous. It is known that in 1826-27, two hundred and five men and six women were murdered by different gangs in Malwah and Rajpootana. In 1827-28, three hundred and sixty-four males and twenty-one females were strangled in Kandeish, Berar, and Guzerat. In 1828-29, two hundred and twenty-six men and six women were thus disposed of in Malwah and Kandeish. In 1829-30, ninety-four men, four women, and a child perished in Baroda and Bundlecund. In 1830-31 the Bundlecund gangs destroyed fifty-seven males and one female. In 1830-31-32, one hundred and seventy males and five females were murdered in Rajpootana and Guzerat. And in 1832-33, forty-one males were strangled in the Gwalior district alone. It has been estimated that on an average more than ten distinct cases of murder occurred in every expedition, and that every Thug went upon at least ten expeditions, which would assign to each a guilty complicity in fully one hundred murders. The amount of property of which they despoiled the public must also have been very great, and occasionally individual prizes were of no trivial value. Thus in 1826 a party of fourteen were murdered by a gang of one hundred and fifty Thugs, and a booty secured worth £2,500. In 1827, seven men were murdered by three hundred and fifty Thugs, and robbed of £2,200. In 1828, the murder of nine persons by a gang of one hundred and twenty-five yielded £4,000; and in 1829, that of six persons produced £8,200, to be divided between one hundred and fifty Thugs.

It must seem incredible, but it is nevertheless the simple fact, that this terrible system of murder flourished for nearly two centuries under those native governments of whose excellence so much has been said in certain quarters. The division of the vast peninsula into many separate, independent, and jealous states, no doubt, encouraged the perpetration of crime by facilitating escape and rendering detection and apprehension almost impossible. So long as their own subjects or tenants were not molested, neither princes nor landed proprietors considered themselves bound to interfere with an institution of which they entertained a mysterious dread, and whence they derived goodly gifts and a handsome revenue. Superstition and cupidity were powerful allies in favour of the Thugs, who, besides, in their palmy days, exhibited admirable prudence and tact in avoiding whatever might be offensive to their patrons and injurious to themselves. They were especially careful not to touch any European, for they well knew that from such they were more likely to receive lead than gold, and that search would be made for the missing man; nor, indeed, was the like facility afforded for familiarity, owing, in a great measure, as Fuseli would say, to "de d—d ignorance of de language." All tell-tale property they quickly destroyed, and never committed a murder near home, or where they were known; nor after a murder did they ever proceed in the direction whence their victims had come, lest they should be betrayed by a horse, a bullock, or an ass, being anywhere recognised. The native custom of sending remittances in the form of jewels and precious metals without any armed escort, and of carrying considerable sums upon the person, increased the temptation of doing honour to Bhowanee. The vast population, too, was always in motion. Parties of travellers, or lonely wanderers, on foot, or on horseback, streamed along the roads and bye-paths, reposing in the intense heat of the day or during the moonless hours of the night beneath the hospitable shade of a grove of mangoes and other stately trees, or around the well that owed its origin to pious vanity. And the very terror felt for their unknown enemies made the travellers an easier prey, for in seeking to avoid the danger, they frequently ran into it by inviting the company of the mild, cheerful and intelligent companions, who were ever ready to converse with them, to walk with them, and—to murder them. Their existence was first known to the English in 1799, after the fall of Seringapatam, when a hundred Phanseegars, or Thugs, were taken prisoners at Bangalore, though even then they were not suspected of pursuing an hereditary profession. The first regular information concerning their habits was not obtained until 1807, when a gang of them was arrested between Chittore and Arcot. It had frequently been remarked, indeed, that very many sepoys never returned to their regiments on the expiration of their leave of absence, and they were struck off the rolls as deserters. But when the true cause of their absence was discovered, the Commander-in-Chief,

Major-General St. Leger, issued a general order in 1810, warning the native troops against associating with chance companions on the road, and advising them to send their money to their homes by means of *hoondees*, or bills, and not to travel by night. The evil, however, was of too monstrous a growth to be thus easily checked. And there was likewise great difficulty experienced in bringing home any particular crime, even when the perpetrators happened to be in custody. The merchants and bankers whose property had been stolen were reluctant to appear in court to give evidence: it was looked upon as somewhat of an indignity, and the cautious delays of English jurisprudence caused a waste of time they could ill endure. Their money was gone, and there was an end of it. It was predestined that it should go in that manner. The thieves were merely instruments working out the will of Providence. Against them they bore no malice or vindictive feeling. Even the relatives of murdered men refused to come forward until they obtained a promise that they should not be summoned to appear in a distant court. And in the majority of cases it was impossible to ascertain who were the murdered persons, or whence they came. A few isolated cases of conviction did, indeed, occur, as in 1823, when Mr. Molony arrested a gang of 115 in the valley of the Nerbudda, and convicted the whole of them; and again in 1826, when a large gang was arrested in the same valley by Major Wardlaw, and their guilt proven. But these exceptions rather tended to make the Thugs more cautious than to induce them to relinquish their ancestral vocation. It was not until 1829-30 that the task of suppression was fairly commenced. The honour of the initiative was reserved for Lord William Bentinck, who passed certain acts rendering Thuggee the object of a special judicature, and giving a wider discretion to the officers employed in its suppression. His lordship was fortunate in his selection of the special officers. It is needless to do more than mention the names of the late Major General, then Captain, Sleeman, Major, now Colonel, Borthwick, Colonel Stewart, Captain Patton, Captain Malcolm, Captain G. Hollings, and Mr. F. C. Smith. The best proof of the ability and energy displayed by these gentlemen is the fact that by the year 1840 the committals amounted to 3,689. Of this number, 466 were hanged, 1,504 transported, 933 imprisoned for life, 81 confined for different periods, 86 called upon to give ample security for their future good conduct, 97 acquitted, and 56 admitted as approvers: 12 effected their escape, and 208 died a natural death before sentence was passed. The approvers were not absolutely pardoned, or even released from custody. Sentence was passed upon them in the usual manner, but respited as long as they showed signs of repentance and reformation. The utmost caution was used in sifting their evidence and in confronting them with the accused, but their testimony was so clear and so thoroughly substantiated that no reasonable man could entertain the slightest doubt as to their veracity. So complete was the success of the measures now adopted that on the 17th of August, 1840, Hoossain Dost Khan, a powerful Talooqdar (baronial lord) in the Nizam's dominions, previously an avowed opponent of the British, wrote a letter to Captain Malcolm, from which the following is an extract:—"Seeing that the best arrangements have been made in this matter, the whole of the inhabitants of the country, and travellers, have been emancipated from the fear of Thugs; day and night they raise their hands in prayer to state that in the days of kings bygone no such peace and comfort existed. Thanks to Almighty God, the power of conferring this great boon, a source of great renown has been reserved for you from the beginning of the world, in order that this matter should be so arranged. Where are the murdered men? How can there be any, when you do not even hear the slightest allusion to Thugs? The whole world are giving thanks for this." It must be confessed, however, that there was some slight exaggeration in the worthy Talooqdar's congratulations, for in the course of the next seven years 531 more Thugs were apprehended and committed for trial. Of these, 33 were hanged, 174 transported, 267 imprisoned for life and 27 for shorter periods, 5 called upon to put in bail, 125 acquitted, and 46 admitted as approvers: besides 11 who died, and 2 who made their escape. It was no easy matter to prevent the last contingency, so great was their patience and ingenuity. Towards the close of 1834, twenty-seven prisoners escaped from the Jubbulpore gaol, by cutting through their irons and the bars of their windows, with thread smeared with oil and then incrusted with finely-powdered stone. In 1848 also there were 120 committed, of whom 5 were hanged, 24 transported, 11 imprisoned for life and 31 for a limited period, 7 required to find substantial bail, 12 acquitted, and 9 admitted as approvers: 2 died, and 10 remained under trial. Since that year Thuggee appears to have quite died out. In 1853, indeed, some cases occurred in the Punjaub, but vigorous measures being at once adopted, under the superintendence of Captain Sleeman, whose happy lot it was to complete the good work inaugurated by his distinguished father, its final suppression was almost coincident with its revival.

The question that next presented itself for the anxious consideration of the Government was the means of providing for the families of the approvers. If left to their own devices, or the suggestions of want, there was too much reason to apprehend that the elder members, who had already witnessed the taking of human life, might be tempted to revert to the practices of their forefathers. Accordingly, in the year 1838, on the recommendation of Captain Charles Brown, a School of Industry was founded at Jubbulpore, for the purpose of teaching the sons of the approvers a trade or craft by which they might earn an honest livelihood. At first their parents were opposed to the idea, but soon joyfully acquiesced when they came to understand the benevolent motives of the Government. For a time the old Thugs continued to speak with animation of their past achievements, but, gradually weaned from their former habits and associations, they learned to look back with shame upon their antecedents and studiously avoided any further allusion to them. By the end of 1847 the school possessed 850 inmates, of whom 307 were employed as guards, brickmakers, builders, cleaners, &c., &c.; while the remaining 543 applied their superior ingenuity to the manufacture of lac dye, sealing-wax, blankets, *satringees* (a sort of strong drugget), fine cloth for trousers, *dhotees*, or body cloths, *newar* tape of sorts, cotton wicks, stockings, gloves, towels, tents, and carpeting. In that year the product of their labour amounted to 131 tents, 3324 yards of Kidderminster carpeting, forty-six woollen carpets, and a vast quantity of towels, table-cloths, plaids, checks, &c., which realised upwards of £3,500. Of this sum £500 were given to the Thugs as an encouragement, and to form a capital for such as were allowed after a time to establish themselves in Jubbulpore on their own account. And nearly £300 were paid to their wives for spinning thread for the factory. Much of the success of this institution has no doubt been due to the excellent and judicious superintendence of Mr. Williams, formerly a patrol of the Delhi Customs.

Let British supremacy in India cease when it will, the suppression of Thuggee will ever remain a glorious monument to the zeal, energy, and judgment of the civil and military servants of the East India Company. It is easy to direct epigram and inuendo against the idea of a body of merchants ruling a vast empire with enlightened and disinterested beneficence. But the impartial student of Anglo-Indian history can readily adduce many such examples as the preceding — for instance, the suppression of Suttee, human sacrifices, and infanticide; the repression of torture, gang robberies, and voluntary mutilation—in order to prove that these merchants were truly princes, these traffickers the honourable of the earth.

The Tusma-Baz Thugs.

The Tusma-Baz Thugs were the fruit of European civilization grafted on the Asiatic stock. At the commencement of the present century one Creagh, a private in an English regiment stationed at Cawnpore, initiated three natives of low degree into the mysteries of an art, formerly practised by thimble-riggers in this country, and known as "pricking the garter." The game, designated Tusma-bazee by his Hindoo disciples, was played in this manner:—a strap being doubled into many folds, the bystanders were requested to insert a stick where the first double took place, which it was impossible to do without the consent of the juggler. Creagh's three apostles speedily became the leaders of as many schools or gangs, numbering in the year 1848, when they were brought to justice, about fifty persons, chiefly residing in the outskirts of Cawnpore. They had long been known to the police authorities as professional gamblers, and had more than once been either punished for that offence or required to furnish security for their good behaviour. It was not their custom, however, to confine their depredations to their native town. On the contrary, they travelled to a considerable distance to the westward, preferring those districts which still remained under the misrule of petty independent princes. Their first proceeding was to conciliate the police, which was usually effected by the promise of one-fourth of their profits. Having thus provided against all chance of molestation, they would meet as strangers, and accidentally, near some well frequented spot, and gradually begin to play. By degrees a crowd gathered around them, and some one or another was certain to be tempted to try his fortune. At first he was, of course, allowed to win, but it rarely happened that he finally escaped being fleeced of his last coin. The leader received a double share of the plunder, in consideration of the risk and expence he incurred in maintaining his followers until a sufficient booty had been secured to render them independent. If any one of the gang was arrested, it was the leader's duty to use every means in his power to release him, and for every rupee he expended for this purpose he was allowed two pice interest. The balance, after deducting the captain's share was equally divided among the rest, and was generally squandered in drinking and gambling among themselves. It was, however, a light and lucrative profession, and they frequently remitted considerable sums of money to their families. But they did not solely rely on their superior sleight of hand. When the opportunity was favourable they did not scruple to add murder to robbery. Their ordinary plan seems to have been by means of medicated sweetmeats, or sugar, hospitably pressed upon the unwary who ventured to test their skill in play. The drug mostly used was expressed from the seed of the *datura* plant, a powerful and dangerous narcotic. To call them Thugs was evidently a misnomer, for they had none of the observances of that ancient fraternity, nor did they lay any claim to religious motives. They were simply organized bands of vagrants of the most worthless characters, who preferred fraud to labour and murder to industry. Their detection would have taken place at a much earlier period, had not the police been bribed to connive at their proceedings. It is almost superfluous to remark that their practices were no sooner discovered by the European magistrates than their occupation was gone, and themselves severely punished.

Dacoits, or Gang-Robbers of India.

In India, under its native rulers, murder and robbery were hereditary professions. The Thugs, or hereditary murderers, have been completely put down; but the work of suppression has not yet been equally successful with regard to the hereditary robbers, as they ever found a ready harbour of refuge in the waste lands of the late kingdom of Oude, and, indeed, in every independent state. They usually lived in colonies, in the midst of wild jungles, difficult of access. With incredible rapidity they would sweep down on some distant town or village, plunder some house previously selected for the purpose, and before any pursuit could be organized they were far advanced on their homeward journey. To avert suspicion they assumed various disguises with admirable adaptability. North of the Jumna they generally travelled as holy-water carriers, because long files of that class of men were continually traversing the roads of that district. But to the south of the Jumna they appeared as

Brinjaras, or drivers of laden bullocks, or as pilgrims journeying to some sacred shrine, or as sorrowing relatives conveying the bones of the departed to the banks of the Ganges; or as the friends of a bridegroom going to fetch home his bride. In the funeral processions to the "holy Gunga," men's bones were borne in red, those of women in white bags, neither of which were ever allowed to touch the earth, but at their halting grounds were suspended from the apex of a triangle formed by three short poles or staves. These were afterwards useful to the Dacoits as handles for the spear-heads which they carried in their waist-bands. Instead of the bones of their parents they contented themselves with those of inferior animals, wild or domestic. The chief advantage of this disguise was that such mourners were every where treated with the utmost respect, and never subjected to inconvenient inquiries as to whence they came or whither they were going. In Central India a more successful mummery was to assume the garb and appearance of Alukramies, a peculiar class of pilgrims, who travelled in small parties accompanying a high-priest—personated by the leader of the gang. "They had four or five tents, some of white and some of dyed cloth, and two or three pairs of Nakaras, or kettle-drums, and trumpets, with a great number of buffaloes, cows, goats, sheep, and ponies. Some were clothed, but the bodies of the greater part were covered with nothing but ashes, paint, and a small cloth waist-band. Those who had long hair went bare-headed, and those who had nothing but short hair wore a piece of cloth round the head." The pretended Alukramies always took the precaution of hiring the services of half a dozen genuine Byragees, or ascetics, whom they put forward in difficult emergencies. They would often stop for days together in one place, awaiting favourable tidings from the scouts they sent out in all directions. On arriving at a village the drums were beat and the trumpets sounded to announce their approach, and some of the party were sent in, with silver sticks, in the name of the high-priest to bring the headman to pay his respects and offer the established Nuzzurana of 1¼ rupee (two shillings and sixpence). If this offering were not punctually and promptly made, double the amount was exacted on the following day, and he must have been a bold man who would venture, by a refusal, to incur the displeasure of the gods. The landholder, or proprietor of the village, was also expected to furnish, gratuitously, a sufficient number of men to carry the tents, flags, drums, and trumpets of these pious cormorants, whose demands, however, were usually complied with without a murmur. They were distinguished from other wandering mendicants by "a large red flag upon a long pole, with the figure of Hunooman, or the Sun and Moon, embroidered upon it. On one occasion they (the Dacoits) prevailed upon Cheytun Das, a celebrated Byragee of Hindoon in Jyepore, then eighty years of age, to enact the high priest, and he was accompanied by his chief disciple, or son, Gunga Das."

There were various clans, or colonies, of Dacoits. The Budhuks lived in the Oude Teraie, or belt of forest land lying along the foot of the Nepaul hills, whence they made frequent incursions into the British territory, especially to the eastward in the direction of Goruckpore. They were men of low caste, and would eat anything but bullocks, cows, buffaloes, snakes, foxes, and lizards. Agricultural employments they abhorred as too toilsome. According to a familiar proverb, "once a Budhuk, always a Budhuk, and all Budhuks are Dacoits." Their leaders were almost invariably men of good descent: some of them affected to trace back their ancestors for twenty generations, and adduced their long impunity as a proof that they were predestined to be what they were, and that, consequently they could never be anything else. "The tiger's offspring," they would say, "are tigers—the young Budhuks become Dacoits." In their palmy days they were able to maintain ten or a dozen wives, but when misfortunes came upon them they were compelled to reduce the pleasing burden to four or five. And they were not altogether a burden, for each wife received in the division of spoil a sum equal to two-thirds of her husband's share. A penitent Budhuk once made the logical, but ungallant remark, that it was the women who ought to be transported, for then no more Budhuks would be born into the world. Nevertheless, in times of trouble the old women were not without their use. They would then assume the semblance of extreme poverty, and, mounted on wretched ponies, would travel many a long weary mile to the place where their relatives were confined, and by judicious presents to the native officers in authority, generally succeeded in mitigating the lot, if they failed to accomplish the release, of the prisoners. In this labour of love they not unfrequently expended between one and two hundred pounds. There were also Budhuks by adoption, but these were never allowed to eat with the hereditary robbers, though they might smoke the same hookah. As a matter of choice they preferred to avoid bloodshed, but in self-defence, or to secure the success of their attack they never scrupled either to wound or to slay outright. Shoojah-ood-Dowlah, Nawab of Oude, once attempted to direct their love of enterprise into an honorable channel by enrolling 1,200 of them into a corps. commanded by their own leaders. But their depredations became so intolerable that they acquired the appropriate epithet of the "Wolf Regiment," and as they were continually mutinying they were soon afterwards disbanded. A brief narrative of a few cases of Dacoitee committed by the Budhuks will give the best idea of the system they pursued.

In the early part of 1818 a powerful gang started from Khyradee in Oude with the intention of cutting off a treasure, escorted by sixty armed police, on the way from Benares to the westward. They disguised themselves as bird-catchers and took with them "falcons and hawks of all kinds, well trained, also mynas, parrots, and other kinds of speaking and mocking birds." They had also a boat prepared to convey them across the river. Having learnt from their scouts that the treasure would be lodged on a particular night in the Chobee-ka-Serai between

Allahabad and Cawnpore, they fitted handles to their axes and spear-heads, and made some rude ladders by means of which, about two hours after dark, they scaled the wall of the Serai. "A guard which had been told off for the purpose broke open the gate from the inside and stood over it to prevent any attack from without, or escape from within, while the rest attacked the escort and secured the treasure." In this spirited affair the Dacoits killed eight and wounded seventeen of the police, carried off £7,600 in specie, and made their escape without the loss of a single man.

In April of the same year the Governor of Bharaitch forwarded to the General Treasury at Lucknow the sum of £2,600 in silver and £600 in gold mohurs, in two carts, escorted by thirty soldiers of the royal army. It was lodged, for one night, outside the gate of a small fort, two loaded guns commanding the only approach. A noted leader, named Naeka, with a gang of eighty Dacoits undertook to cut out the prize. First of all, he divided his followers into three parties. One division of twenty men rushed upon the guns and spiked them. A second, of equal force, fastened the gate of the fort with a strong chain to prevent the garrison from sallying forth; while the others boldly attacked the guard and killed four of them—two of their own party, however, being wounded. As they were returning in hot haste to their homes they were themselves assailed by two large land owners, who took from them £2,000 in rupees and the whole of the gold. They in their turn fell into the hands of the king's troops—Naeka and sixty of his associates being also apprehended. After six years' detention in the Seetapore gaol they were all released, the land-owners paying a fine of £2,000 in addition to their booty, and the Dacoits a further sum of £1,000.

Fortune, certainly, did not always smile upon them, notwithstanding her proverbial partiality for the brave. Two gangs having united one day in May, 1819, attacked the house of Sah Beharee Lall, a rich banker, residing in the heart of Lucknow, the capital city of Oude. At first all went well with them, and they carried off upwards of £4,000 into a jungle not far from Khyrabad. A dispute then arose among the leaders respecting the division of the plunder, and one of them, thinking himself unjustly treated, rode off to Lucknow and gave information that led to the apprehension of two hundred men, women, and children. A long and tedious imprisonment awaited them, until in despair they rose upon their guard, in 1834, and seventy of them effected their escape, leaving five of their comrades on the ground, two of them being killed upon the spot. The others were released in 1839.

The boldness and suddenness of their onset usually assured their success. One evening in the month of February, 1822, a party of men, carrying canes in their hands, and about forty in number, were observed hurrying along in a loose straggling manner towards the military station of Nursingpore. On reaching the rivulet that separates the town from the cantonments they were challenged by the sentry—for a picket of soldiers was always posted on the bank, under a native officer. Carelessly answering that they were cowherds and that their cattle were coming on after them, they proceeded without molestation up the principal street, but suddenly halted in front of a shop of some pretensions. Striking their torches against pots containing combustible matter, with which they had previously provided themselves, they were instantly surrounded with a blaze of light. Already bewildered, the bystanders were terrified into silence by a few rapid thrusts of the spears, into which the canes had been instantaneously transformed. The house was rifled as if by magic, ten or a dozen persons were killed or wounded, and in a quarter of an hour from their entrance into the town, the Dacoits were on their way to the jungles. Within twenty paces on one side of the house was a police station, and not a hundred paces on the other side was the picket of sepoys already alluded to. But as marriage processions were just then of frequent occurrence, it was supposed that the noise and the glare of the torches belonged to those very uproarious festivities, until a little boy creeping along a ditch whispered to the native officer that they had killed his father. The alarm was immediately given, but before the troops could turn out, the Dacoits had got a fair start, which carried them beyond the reach of both horse and foot.

A bolder exploit was performed towards the close of that year. Two skilful leaders, having collected some forty followers and distributed among them ten matchlocks, ten swords, and twenty-five spears, waylaid a treasure going from the native Collector's treasury at Budrauna to Goruckpore. The prize consisted of £1,200, and was guarded by a Naik, or corporal, with four sepoys and five troopers. It had to pass through a dense jungle, and it was settled—said one of them in after years—"that the attack should take place there; that we should have strong ropes tied across the road in front and festooned to trees on both sides, and, at a certain distance behind, similar ropes festooned to trees on one side, and ready to be fastened on the other, as soon as the escort of horse and foot should get well in between them." Having completed these preparations the gang laid down on either side of the road patiently awaiting their prey. "About five in the morning," continued the narrator, "we heard a voice as if calling upon the name of God (Allah), and one of the gang started up at the sound and said, 'Here comes the treasure!' We put five men in front with their matchlocks loaded not with ball but shot, that we might, if possible, avoid killing anybody. When we had got the troopers, infantry, and treasure all within the space, the hind ropes were run across the road and made fast to the trees on the opposite side, and we opened a fire in upon the party from all sides. The foot soldiers got into the jungle at the sides of the road, and the troopers tried to get over the ropes at both ends, but in vain." The corporal and a horse were killed, two troopers wounded, and the treasure carried off in spite of a hot pursuit.

One of the most famous Budhuk chiefs was named Maherban, who lived in his fort at Etwa in the Oude forest. He had seven wives, who frequently accompanied him in his expeditions, with the exception of his chief wife, from whom no such toils and risk were expected. Late in the autumn of 1818 he and his brother assembled about two hundred men, women, and children, and wisely settled beforehand the rates of division of plunder, setting aside a portion for the families of those who might die or be killed. They then sacrificed ten goats, and, each dipping a finger into the blood, swore mutual fidelity; after which they ate and drank and made merry. On the following evening Maherban and twenty of the principal Dacoits advanced a little way in front of the rest of the party, and spat in the direction they were about to pursue. Then raising his hands towards heaven Maherban thus prayed aloud:—"If it be thy will, O God! and thine, O Kalee! to prosper our undertaking, for the sake of the blind and the lame, the widow and the orphan, who depend upon our exertions for subsistence, vouchsafe, we pray thee, the call of the female jackal!" His followers likewise lifted up their hands, and having repeated the prayer after their leader, all sat down in attentive silence. The auspicious omen was presently heard three times upon the left. Thus assured of success, Maherban purchased a palanquin for his second wife—suitable for a man of wealth and dignity. The gang now started for Benares in small detachments, and took lodgings in different parts of that city where they stayed a whole month, making offerings and inquiries. Intelligence was at length received of a cartload of treasure going towards the west, under the care of an armed police force. On the first night of December the escort rested with their precious charge in a public Serai at Josee near Allahabad. Having procured staves for their spears and handles for their axes, the gang left the palanquin, their wives, and superfluous clothes, in a grove about four miles distant. At midnight they arrived at the Serai and were agreeably surprised to find the gate open. Here one detachment halted and mounted guard, while another overawed the police, and the rest plundered the treasure. A brave merchant, named Kaem Khan, likewise reposing in the Serai, in vain endeavoured to infuse courage into the panic-stricken escort by word and gesture. Disgusted with their pusillanimity he continued to lay about him with his long straight sword, wounding two of his assailants and severing in twain many a spear, until a Dacoit got behind him and felled him with a bludgeon, when he was quickly put to death. They then carried off twenty bags containing in all 14,000 Spanish dollars, and had their wounded men tended at a neighbouring village. As some compensation for their sufferings they presented each of them with £10 in addition to his share.

A career of triumph had the same effect upon Maherban as upon greater heroes: it made him indolent and luxurious, and his followers repined at their forced inactivity. "One day, while he was sitting with two of his wives, Mooneea and Soojaneea, they taunted him on the long interval of rest he had enjoyed, while his more active brother had been covering his followers and family with honour and money. 'You have,' said Soojaneea, 'been now some ten months without attempting any enterprise worthy your reputation; you are at your ease, and indulging in sports no doubt very agreeable to you, but without any honour or profit to us, while these your followers, men of illustrious birth and great courage, are suffering from want, and anxiety about their families. They have been told of a boat coming from Calcutta, laden with Spanish dollars; if you do not wish to go yourself and take it, pray lend us your swords, and we will go ourselves, and try what we can do, rather than let your brave fellows starve.' Maherban was deeply stung by these reproaches, and waxed very warm, but was too angry to make any reply to his wives. He got his followers together, and leaving his principal wife, Mooneea, behind him, he set out in the character of a chief of high rank, going on a pilgrimage, with Soojaneea carried in a splendid litter as a princess; and in four months they returned with some 40,000 Spanish dollars." While on his way homewards from this successful expedition he "gave a large sum of money to a gardener at Seosagur, about three miles from Saseram, to plant a grove of mango-trees near a tank, for the benefit of travellers, in the name of Rajah Maherban Sing, of Gour in Oude, and promised him further aid on future occasions of pilgrimage, if he found the work progressing well, saying, 'that it was a great shame that travellers should be left as he had been, without shade for themselves and their families to rest under, during the heat of the day.'" As he approached his forest home all the women went forth to meet him in holiday attire, and welcomed "the conquering hero"—and the dollars—with music and dancing.

Encouraged by this brilliant success Maherban resolved to proceed at the close of the season to Sherghottee to intercept another boat-load of dollars, which his spies told him was to be conveyed from Calcutta to Benares. First of all he engaged a discharged Sepoy to instruct his men in the Company's drill, and very apt scholars they proved themselves. But while this parade work was going on, one of them eloped with Heera Sing's pretty wife. The injured man straightway applied to Maherban for redress, but the chief was too busy with his preparations to attend to a merely personal affair, and probably deemed the loss of a reluctant wife no very serious matter. Heera Sing then betook himself to the other leaders, but failed to enlist their sympathy, for a man who cannot bind a wife by her affections deserves to lose her. Foiled at all points, he determined upon a large and base revenge: he gave information of Maherban's movements to the English magistrates.

Suspecting no treachery, Maherban at length set out as a Hindoo prince with a noble retinue, and attended by a numerous guard of soldiers dressed in the Company's uniform. Unfortunately for him and his followers, the Dacoitee of the previous year had been carefully tracked out and the guilt lodged at the door of the real criminals. Mr. Cracroft, the magistrate of Jaunpore, was accordingly authorized to proceed to surprise his fastness with four companies of native infantry under the command of Captain Anquetil. Their march was unmolested, and in the heart of a dense unhealthy jungle—though not so experienced by the Dacoits themselves—they came upon his fort, a parallelogram sixty yards long by forty wide. It was surrounded by a ditch with an embankment within, formed of the mud there excavated. At a short distance was another colony of about five hundred able-bodied Budhuks governed by Cheyda, Maherban's brother. These united with the few who had been left at home by the latter, and opened a warm but ill-directed fire upon the troops, as they advanced with cheers to the assault. The simple works were carried at the first rush, and whatever was combustible was committed to the flames. But it was impossible to follow up the retreating Dacoits, and having inflicted this trivial injury Captain Anquetil had no alternative but to extricate his detachment from their dangerous position, and return to head-quarters.

Meanwhile measures were taken by the magistrates at Jaunpore, Behar, and Benares, to intercept and arrest the gang under Maherban himself. That chief was artfully induced to leave the high road and make a pilgrimage to Gunga. Here he was given to understand that there was an informality in the payment of customs' dues, and that he must halt until the matter could be adjusted. While encamped in a mango grove he was suddenly surrounded by the police, but still imagining that his apprehension was entirely due to the supposed irregularity, his followers offered no resistance, and only discovered their mistake on being committed for trial as robbers and murderers. Maherban himself was hanged in 1821, and the whole of his gang, 160 in number, imprisoned for life or for limited periods.

After Maherban's execution his principal widow Mooneea succeeded to the government of the survivors of his colony. In the autumn of 1823 the adventurous dame joined some noted leaders in fitting out an expedition, consisting of eighty men and seven women, with the intention of cutting off a treasure party going to Katmandoo. Having taken the auspices in the usual manner, but actually guided by their pre-determination, they moved in small parties towards Junnukpore in the Nepaul territory. While travelling in disguise, some of them fell in with a detachment of eighty Goorkhas (Nepaul highlanders) escorting fifteen bullocks laden with 64,000 rupees (£6,400). Two of them contrived to attach themselves to the escort, while the others separated to collect their comrades. When about fifty had got together they resolved to make the attack without waiting for the others. The guard lodged that night about twelve miles from Jungpore, in a place surrounded by a wall and ditch, outside of which was an encampment of nearly 500 merchants, itinerant traders, and other travellers. The night was clear and bright, but they nevertheless kindled their torches, and with the aid of two stout ladders hastily constructed, effected an entrance, surprised the guard, and possessed themselves of the treasure. It was too cumbersome, however, to be all carried off at once, and they were consequently obliged to bury about 17,000 rupees. The news of this outrage having reached the Nepaul military station of Jalesur, all suspicious persons were detained, and among them some members of the gang who, under the lash, confessed their complicity and led to the arrest of twenty-nine others, and to the death of two, who foolishly resisted. These also being subjected to the lash pointed out the *caches* where the 17,000 rupees had been buried, and 35,000 more were found upon their persons: the others got off with the rest of the treasure. The information obtained from the prisoners furnished the clue to the apprehension of a vast number of Dacoits whom the Oude authorities threw into prison without undergoing even the form of a trial. With like irregularity some of them were released as a *Khyrat*, or "thanksgiving to God," whenever the King or any member of the royal family recovered from an illness.

The scanty remnants of this last gang finding their former fastnesses no longer secure, fled for refuge to the Rajah of Kottar within the British territories, who readily accepted their presents, and in return promised them his protection. From these new head-quarters they frequently sallied forth, and joining their old comrades, made inroads into Rohilcund and the Doab. Being unable to plunder in western Oude, because the landowners in their strongholds defied both king and Dacoits, they confined their depredations to the Company's territories, and so constantly attacked and plundered the treasuries of the native collectors, that the Government was compelled to fortify them and impose a guard. Even this did not always prevail, and large sums of money were oftentimes carried off, after the guard had been surprised and overpowered.

The Budhuks dwelling in the eastern part of the Teraie were better known as Seear Marwars, and were originally husbandmen, but took to Dacoitee in the Nawabship of Shoojah-ood-Doolah. They numbered in all from four to six thousand males, but were divided into colonies of three or four hundred each, clustered round a rude fort. They were in the habit of giving 25 per cent. of their booty to the Zemindars whose protection they enjoyed, and by whom they were generally subsidized to fight their battles with their neighbours, or with the farmers of the revenue. In 1826-27 Mr., now Sir, Frederick Currie, the magistrate of Goruckpore, organised a system of repression by means of a corps of Irregular Cavalry under Major Hawkes, and an augmentation of his own police force. That gentleman flattered himself that he had completely put down this tribe of Dacoits, but, in fact, he had only driven them into another district. Their old haunts no longer sheltering them from pursuit, they removed their household gods to Rohilcund, the Doab ("Mesopotamia"), Rajpootana, and Gwalior. The Budhuk colonies, however distant from one another, kept up an interchange of civilities and intermarried with one another. Members of the same *gote*, or family, though belonging to different colonies, could not intermarry, but as there were several *gotes* in every colony, the different settlements could interchange sons and daughters. For instance Solunkee ("Mr. Brown") could not marry a person of the same name in his own, or in any another colony, but there was no objection to his taking to wife the daughter of Powar ("Mr. Jones,") or Dhundele ("Mr. Robinson") however closely they might be connected with him.

Mr. Currie certainly did succeed in momentarily checking the depredations of the plunderers in his own district, but within three years the evil had returned to its former dimensions. And of these some idea may be formed from the statement that between 1818 and 1834, the Budhuks of the Oude Teraie were known to have committed 118 Dacoitees, in which 172 men were killed, 682 wounded, and property carried off to the value of nearly £115,000: although 457 of the miscreants were arrested, only 186 could be legally convicted. But the actual number of gang-robberies far exceeded that which was reported. Many of the Dacoits boasted that they had been engaged in a dozen or fifteen expeditions. One of them confessed to Mr. Hodgson, in 1824, that he had participated in seven Dacoitees, yielding a total of £36,900. A noted leader, named Lucka, was engaged in forty-nine, in the course of twenty-five years, some of them taking place at a distance of four or five hundred miles from his home. A Chumbul Dacoit confessed to thirty-eight in twenty-seven years, and another to twenty-three in twenty-two years; and another Oude Budhuk to thirty-nine in thirty-three years. They generally commenced at an early age, from eighteen to twenty, according to the vigour of their constitution. Lucka, of whom mention is made above, was arrested under the disguise of a Byragee, his body smeared with ashes and a house of peacock's feathers on his back: but the restlessness of his eye, and the nervous movements of his limbs betrayed him. Arrest and punishment, however, were always endured with commendable resignation, being considered as the accidents of their profession.

The achievements of Bukshee and other leaders soon proved the fallacy of Mr. Currie's complacent belief in the efficacy of his repressive measures. In November, 1830, Bukshee's gang slowly travelled through Oude, in the disguise of

Ganges water-carriers, moving in small parties and encamping in groves to avoid unpleasant interrogatories. Arriving at the frontiers, they gradually concentrated towards Sursole in the Cawnpore district, where they were informed by their spies that a private treasure was on its way from Mirzapore to Furruckabad. Having cut handles for their axe and spear heads, they crossed the Ganges in a boat previously purchased for the occasion, and worked by two well-disposed ferrymen. After reaching the opposite bank they had still ten miles to go, so that it was almost midnight before they attained their destination. A sudden rush was all that was then necessary, though to increase the panic caused by their irruption they deemed it expedient to wound six or seven of the escort. Breaking open the boxes, they abstracted twenty-five bags, each containing 1000 rupees (in all, £2,500), and made off to the river. But by that time it was daylight, and the ferrymen had run their boat under the shelter of a high bank, and were fast asleep. Afraid to make a noise by hallooing to them, the Dacoits buried their treasure in the sands and dispersed themselves among the neighbouring villages until nightfall. In the meantime the police had discovered their boat, but being assured by the men that it had brought over only some fodder for cattle, they immediately gave it up. Soon after sunset the robbers met at the appointed rendezvous, where they found the boatmen anxiously expecting them. So, digging up the treasure, they went on board and were safely ferried over to the other side, presenting each of these men with fifty rupees.

About the same season of the following year Bukshee again took the field in his old disguise, and moved down to Allahabad. This was the place of rendezvous for the different detachments, and here they made their offerings to the gods, and received the blessings of the priests and prayers for success in all their undertakings. They then returned to the left bank and dropped down the river till they came opposite to Bindachul, where there stood a celebrated temple to Davee. Again crossing to the right bank they worshipped at the shrine of the goddess of destruction, and were rewarded for their devotion by the intelligence that a merchant's shop in Mirzapore, only four miles distant, promised a rich booty. Accordingly, so soon as it was dusk they advanced two miles in that direction, and throwing off their disguise concealed themselves in a hollow till past eight o'clock to allow the streets to get empty. Then they hurried on to the town and stopped before the house chosen for their operations, every avenue to which was guarded by parties told off for that purpose. Suddenly lighting their torches they rushed in at the still open door, stabbing and slashing right and left, and carried off between four and five thousand pounds sterling. A few minutes afterwards they were again clear of the town. Returning to their place of concealment they resumed their garments, hastened thence to the river, and presented each of the boatmen with a hundred rupees for conveying them safely across. In due time they reached their forest homes without hurt or molestation. Connected with this expedition there occurred a characteristic incident. To avoid disputes Bukshee had stipulated before hand that he should receive one-fifth of the plunder in addition to his proper portion and the repayment of the outlay he incurred in fitting out and maintaining the gang, in order to ransom his parents who had been detained in the gaol at Lucknow for the last twelve years. He was no doubt sincere in his intention to apply these funds in the manner he had stated, but unhappily he had several wives, who somehow absorbed the whole amount, and his parents accordingly remained in confinement. When reproached with having obtained the money under fraudulent pretences, Bukshee excused himself by the patriotic remark that his father was now too old to be of any service to the colony: he did not, however, offer to refund the eight thousand rupees he had thus obtained.

The Dacoits do not appear to have possessed the honour that is supposed to exist among thieves in so high a degree as the Thugs. A notable instance of the laxity of their mutual engagements was furnished about the same time that Bukshee successfully defrauded his followers. A gang of forty Dacoits, under two brothers, named Hemraj and Mungul Sing, and their cousin Dhurmoo, were lying at Sherghottee, in the hope of intercepting a treasure then on the way from Calcutta to Benares. Here they were joined, much against their inclination, by a party of fourteen under Ghureeba, who threatened to inform against them unless they agreed not only to admit him into partnership, but also to set aside a proportionate share of the plunder for a gang of twenty-five under Bureear, from whom he had recently parted. After considerable altercation Ghureeba carried his point, and the convention was ratified by oaths of mutual fidelity.

Then they all went on together to the village of Dungaen, at the foot of the hills, where they attacked the treasure-party at night, and, after killing four and wounding sixteen of the escort, carried off twenty-eight bags, each containing 2,500 rupees (in all, £6,000). Hemraj and Mungul Sing now adhered so far to their previous engagements, that they allowed to Ghureeba and the absent Bureear the shares to which they were entitled, but refused to burden themselves in behalf of a party who had rendered them no assistance. Ghureeba expostulated with them to no purpose, and declared he would hold them answerable for the whole amount. After some further jangling, it was finally arranged that 30,000 rupees should be buried until Burecar could fetch them himself, and this labour was voluntarily undertaken by Mungul Sing. On their return home, Bureear displayed such indignation at their unfriendly conduct that they were constrained to pacify him with a present of 2,000 rupees, and a month afterwards Mungul Sing and some others set out with him to dig up the treasure. But instead of 30,000, they found only 18,000 rupees. As might be expected, this discovery of the treachery of his associates did not tend to mollify the already exasperated

Bureear. In his wrath he applied for redress to Rajah Gung Sing, of Dhera Jugdeespore, in the kingdom of Oude, and appointed him arbiter. The Rajah proposed to decide the question by an appeal to heaven, and to this Mungul Sing and his party were compelled to assent. A blacksmith was thereupon ordered to make some cannon-balls red hot, and these were placed with tongs on the palms of the suspected persons' hands, defended only by a thin peepul leaf. The ordeal was to carry these balls a certain distance without being burned, but after taking a few paces they all gave in. They were consequently pronounced guilty, and were sentenced to refund the money they had purloined, and to pay a fine of 500 rupees to the Rajah. In default of restitution, they were delivered over in irons to Bureear, who kept them in confinement for several months, and threatened to cut off their ears unless they made good his loss. But, finding that his own followers were opposed to any further severity, he prudently connived at their escape. "The hands of Boohooa, who afterwards rose to the distinction of a leader, still (1849) bear the marks of the burning he got; and, in showing them to me (Captain Sleeman) one day, he confessed that the 'decision of the

F 2

Deity' in that case was a just one; that he had really assisted Mungul Sing in robbing Ghureeba on that occasion of 10,000 rupees, by burying them in a pit at some distance from the rest; and that he, Nundran, and another of the party, afterwards helped themselves to three out of the ten thousand, unknown to Mungul Sing." What became of the two thousand still unaccounted for—the total deficiency being 12,000—he was unable to say.

The same Bukshee, of whom so much has already been said, was informed by his spies, in January, 1833, that the ex-Peishwah Bajee Rao had hoarded a large amount of gold coin at Bithore, on the right bank of the Ganges, not far from Cawnpore. He accordingly assembled a numerous band of Dacoits, who, after receiving their instructions, broke up into small parties, which concentrated at a particular spot at the appointed time. They then boldly stormed the ex-Peishwah's palace, wounded eighteen of his servants, and carried off 50,000 rupees in silver and 15,000 gold mohurs, each worth fifteen rupees. As they approached their homes they were met by their female relatives in triumphant procession, to whom they made a largesse of fifteen mohurs and twenty rupees to lay out in sweetmeats for themselves and their children. On the following day every man in the village received five gold mohurs, seven rupees, and two four-anna pieces (worth sixpence a piece). A series of the most shocking debaucheries ensued, which resulted in the death of Chunda, the second leader of the gang. Six months afterwards the Oude authorities surprised the colony, when Bukshee and a hundred of his followers were put to the sword, and nearly three hundred taken prisoners; a considerable quantity of plunder was seized at the same time. The Budhuks, however, were soon released, and the king even entertained the idea of restoring the recovered property to its rightful owner. But the queen is said to have suggested to his majesty "that if he suffered the ex-Peishwah to recover his property in this way, he would expose himself to a demand from the honourable company for all that had been taken by gangs from the same colonies in their attacks upon numerous public treasuries and private storehouses in all parts of their dominions, and add to the grounds already urged for depriving him of his country; but that if he allowed the property to be quietly, the noise about it would soon cease, while he would escape all further responsibility and odium."

Her majesty's advice was both too prudent and too palatable to be lightly rejected, and the property was, accordingly, "quietly absorbed."

A yet more dashing, though not equally profitable enterprise was that of the famous Budhuk chief, Gujraj, in 1839. In the absence of the Rajah of Jhansi, who had gone with nearly all his armed retainers to a marriage festival in the Duteea Rajah's family, Gujraj, with fifty followers, scaled the wall of that town, attacked the bankers' shops, killed one man and wounded another, and finally got off unmolested with £4,000 worth of plunder. This leader was warmly patronised by the Rajah of Nurwur, who had always half a dozen of his men to guard him while he slept.

In Rajpootana, Gwalior, and Malwa the Dacoits called themselves Bagrees, or Bagorras. This clan numbered about 1,200 families, principally settled, or rather bivouacked, on the banks of the Chumbul. Of their proceedings less is known than concerning those of their Oude brethren. They were greatly favoured by the native princes and powerful landholders, and even when they were seized their punishment seldom went further than a compulsory restitution of the stolen property. They rarely insulted women beyond demanding of them their gold and silver ornaments, and their reckless liberality made them so popular with the poorer classes that when some of the petty princes were urged by the Indian Government to take steps to put down Dacoitee within their respective territories, they excused themselves on the ground that it would cause a revolution. They were, besides, much prized as auxiliaries in the state of perpetual warfare that existed among these independent princes. When the Alwar Chief, in 1783, renounced his allegiance to the Rajah of Jyepore, his sword and shield was Kishna, the great Bagree leader. At a later period, his grandson, Bijee Sing, rendered an important service to the lord of Alwar, for which he received an estate worth 4,000 rupees a year, rent free for ever. The commander of the Jyepoor forces had reduced the Alwar Chief to great straits, when the latter invoked the aid of Bhart Sing and Bijee Sing, who came to his assistance with 500 Bagrees, resolute and well armed men. The Manukpoor Gotra estate was offered as a reward to any one who would assassinate the enemy's leader. The Dacoits accepted the adventure. "Bhart Sing approached the tent at night with only four or five followers, whom he left outside. He entered the tent, and found the minister asleep and entirely defenceless. He could not kill a man in that state, and taking up his sword, shield, and turban, which lay by the bedside, he returned with them to Bijee Sing, saying that he could never stab a brave man in that defenceless state. Bijee Sing then went, entered the tent which was still without a sentry, and stabbed the minister to the heart."

At another time the Rajah of Kerowlie engaged a small band of Bagrees to assist him in besieging his cousin the Thakoor Luchmun Sing, in the city of Ameergur. "The duty assigned to us"—said one of them—"was to cut off all supplies, and at night to attack the advanced batteries thrown out by the garrison upon elevated places. The commandant allowed us to select as many as we wanted of his best soldiers on whose courage we could most rely, and we generally took about the same number as we ourselves. We then reconnoitred the strongest batteries, sometimes in the daytime in all manner of disguises, sometimes at night creeping along the ground like wild animals, till we got up close to them, and saw all that we wanted to see. After we had become well acquainted with the positions, in three or four days we entered upon the attack.

Well armed with swords, shields, and spears, and some with muskets, we advanced close to the ground till we got so near that we could rush in upon them before the enemy could deliver their fire. No man is permitted to carry a matchlock on such occasions; nor do we, indeed, ever carry them in our enterprises, because the light of the matches might warn people of our approach and bring their fire upon us. When within the proper distance the signal is given, and we start up, and rush in, and kill every man we can. There are always supporting parties of troops close behind us, to follow up our attack and keep possession of the surprised batteries. In this way we in one night surprised and took three of the batteries which Luchmun Sing had placed upon a hill near his fort. The night was dark, and we attacked them all at the same time. We were about forty Bagrees, and we had with us about sixty select soldiers, and for each battery we had from thirty to thirty-five men; but we knew every inch of the ground we were to act upon, and we could rely upon each other. We on such occasions stop all supplies that they try to get into the besieged fort. We watch for several nights and permit the people to take in all they please unmolested; and when we know all the roads by which the supplies go in, we attack them all in one night, and are allowed to keep what we get for ourselves."

These Bagrees were as scrupulously devout in their way as the Italian banditti are said to be, whom they resembled in more than one point. Ajeet Sing, the leader of a Chumbul gang, in describing a Dacoitee that had yielded 40,000 rupees, went on to say:—"Four thousand five hundred rupees were taken to cover the expenses of the road, to offer to the gods who had guided us, and to give in charity to the poor. For offerings to the gods we purchase goats, sweet cakes, and spirits; and having prepared the feast, we throw a handful of the savoury food upon the fire in the name of the gods who have most assisted us; but of the feast so consecrated, no female but a virgin can partake. The offering is made through the man who has successfully invoked the god on that particular occasion; and as my god had guided us on this, I was employed to prepare the feast for him, and to throw the offering on the fire. The offering must be taken up before the feast is touched, and put upon the fire, and a little water must be sprinkled upon it. The savoury smell of the food as it burns, reaches the nostrils of the god and delights him. On this, as on most occasions, I invoked the spirit of Gunga Sing, my grandfather, and to him I made the offering. I considered him to be the greatest of all my ancestors as a robber, and him I invoked on this trying occasion. He never failed me when I invoked him, and I had the greatest confidence in his aid. The spirits of our ancestors can easily see whether we shall succeed in what we are about to undertake; and when we are to succeed, they order us on,—and when we are not, they make signs to us to desist."

The same Ajeet Sing described a singular superstition that existed among the Bagrees. One of his comrades happened to be severely wounded on the wrist, and became so faint from loss of blood that he was obliged to be carried. As he passed under a Banyan tree, "the spirit of the place fell upon him, and the four men who carried him fell down with the shock." The phenomenon was thus explained. "If any man who has been wounded on the field of battle, or in a Dacoitee, be taken bleeding to a place haunted by a spirit, the spirit gets very angry and lays hold of him: he comes upon him in all manner of shapes, sometimes in that of a buffalo, at others in that of a woman, sometimes in the air above, and sometimes from the ground below; but no one can see him except the wounded person he is angry with and wants to punish. Upon such a wounded person we always place a naked sword, or some other sharp steel instrument, as spirits are much afraid of weapons of this kind. If there be any good conjuror at hand to charm the spirits away from the person wounded, he recovers, but nothing else can save him. When the spirit seized Gheesa under the tree, we had unfortunately no conjuror of this kind, and he, poor fellow! died in consequence. It was evident that a spirit had got hold of him, for he could not keep his head upright; it always fell down upon his right or left shoulder as often as we tried to put it right, and he complained much of a pain in the region of the liver. We therefore concluded the spirit had broken his neck, and was consuming his liver."

Dead bodies were usually burned, and the ashes thrown into the sacred stream. Sometimes this could not be done, as, for instance, when one died upon an expedition, and there was no time or means to make a funeral pyre. In such cases the body would be hastily buried, or, as once occurred, thrust into a porcupine's hole, and some of the fingers cut off and carried home to the sorrowing relatives. The part was then burned for the whole, and the gang presented a widow with money to distribute in alms, and enabled her to make a handsome offering to the family priest. Each colony had two or three especial deities, who were the spirits of ancestors distinguished in the "imperial business," as they proudly designated their vocation. When they desired to know who of their forefathers was the most sympathetic, the most interested in their welfare, they carefully noted the incoherent ravings of a delirious man, or one suffering from epilepsy. His rambling talk was attributed to the temporary possession of his tongue by some departed spirit. If there were any doubt as to whose it was, the family priest, or a relative of the sick man, would throw on the ground a few grains of wheat, or coloured glass beads, mentioning the name of some ancestor, and at the same time crying odd or even. If they cried correctly two or three times consecutively, they had discovered the demigod. They then sacrificed a goat, or some other animal, that the pleasant odour of the culinary operations might gratify the nostrils of the "daimon," while the assembled friends loudly sang his praises. If the patient began to amend during the sacrifice, it was deemed a full confirmation of their belief, and a new "Lar familiaris," or household god was added to the polytheism of the colony.

The chief deities worshipped by the Dacoits in common were Kalee or Davee, and Sooruj Deota or Sun God. Before setting out upon an expedition, they were always careful to take the auspices; which was done in this manner. Having procured several goats, the principal men assembled, and while one of them held some water in his mouth, the others prayed, "O thou Sun God! And O all ye other gods! if we are to succeed in the enterprise we are about to undertake, we pray ye to cause these goats to shake their bodies!" If they do not shake them after the gods have been thus duly invoked, the enterprise must not be entered upon, and the goats are not sacrificed. We then try the auspices with the wheat; we have a handful of wheat, a large shell, a brass jug, cloth, and frankincense (*gogul*), and scented wood (*dhoop*) to burn. We burn the frankincense and scented wood, and blow the shell; and taking out a pinch of the grains, put them on the cloth and count them. If they come up odd, the omen is favourable; if even, it is bad. After this, which we call the auspices of the Akut, we take that of the Seearnee, or female jackal. If it calls on the left, it is good; if on the right, it is bad. If the omens turn out favourable in all three trials then we have no fear whatever; but if they are favourable in only one trial out of the three, the enterprise must be given up."

The Bowrees appear to have been an off-set of the Bagree Dacoits. They affected to be descended from Rajpoots, but in truth very little is known as to their origin. Their peculiar dialect, however, was Guzerattee, though for generations past they had not even visited that province, but the circumstance is in favour of the theory that traces them to Chittore, the capital of Mewar, adjacent to Guzerat, whence they are believed to have emigrated when Akhbar captured that city in 1567. According to the deposition of Dhokul Sing, made in 1839, the Bowrees were "not a people of yesterday—we are of ancient and illustrious descent." Their ancestor, Pardhee, was one of the companions of Ram in his expedition for the recovery of Seeta. "If," said this approver, "if any prince happens to have an enemy that he wishes to have made away with, he sends for some of our tribe, and says, 'Go, and bring such or such an one's head.' We go, and steal into his sleeping apartments, and take off the person's head without any other person knowing anything about it. If the prince wanted, not the head of his enemy, but the gold tassels of the bed on which he lay asleep, we brought them to him. In consequence of our skill in these matters, we were held everywhere in high esteem; and we served princes and had never occasion to labour at tillage. We who came to the Delhi territory (they were mostly located about Delhi, Mozuffernugur, and Meerut), and were called Bowrees, took to thieving. Princes still employed us to take off the heads of their enemies, and rob them of their valuables. At present the Bowrees confine themselves almost exclusively to robbing tents; they do not steal cattle, or cut into ("dig through") houses; but they will rob a cart on the highway occasionally—any other trade than robbery they never take to." During the absence of the men on some thriving expedition, their wives and families were protected and maintained by the Zemindar, on whose land they resided, and who likewise was ever ready to advance a small sum of money to enable his respectable tenants to take to the road—secure of repayment with usury. Before setting out they sacrificed a goat to Davee, and offered burnt offerings.

They also presented sweetmeats to the goddess, and vowed no stinted quantity should they return successful from their wanderings. To omens they paid great regard. A couplet in familiar use among them was to the effect, that "if the cow and the deer cross from the left to the right, and the snake from right to left, and the blue jay from left to right, even the wealth that has gone from thee shall come back."

Of the cognate tribes of Sanseea and Bereca Dacoits some interesting details may be gathered from the official reports of the Commissioners for the suppression of Dacoitee. According to tradition there lived a long time ago, in the province or Mharwar, two uterine brothers named Sains Mull and Mullanoor. Sains was very illiterate and found it extremely difficult to earn a livelihood by his own exertions. So he went to the god Bhugwan and represented his case. The deity heard him with compassion and gave him an order upon every village in the world for the payment of half a crown from each. Returning home the foolish fellow showed the paper to his brother, who, moved by envy, tore it in pieces.

A fraternal squabble naturally ensued, which at length terminated by both of them repairing to Bughwan. But the god declined to give a second order, and advised Mullanoor to assume the life of a mendicant, while his brother was to maintain himself by singing and dancing. From the former were descended the Bereeas, who wandered about the country, playing the *dhol* (a kind of drum), begging and stealing: the men and women living together in a promiscuous state of extreme socialism. The descendents of the other brother were called Sanseeas, also a roving tribe, pretending to deal in cattle, goats, horses, cloth, grain, or anything else that came into their hands. They were generally in great request as *Bhâts*, or Bards at the marriage festivals of the Jats. Their business was to trace the lineage of their entertainer to the founders of the Jat family, and celebrate the heroic virtues of his ancestors. If the host proved a niggard, and refused to comply with the exorbitant demands of these vagabond minstrels, they would make an effigy of his father and parade it up and down before his house;—or even, in extreme cases, suspend it from a bamboo and fix it over his door, by which means he temporarily lost caste, so that none of his neighbours would drink or smoke with him. In former times these Bhats almost lived upon the Jats; each claiming, as his peculiar province, fifty or a hundred families who, in succession, gave him yearly one day's food and two shillings and sixpence in money. The Sanseeas were divided into two sub-clans, the Malhas and the Kalkas—the former being descended from Sains Mull's son, and the latter from his grand-daughter by an adopted son. A Malha could not marry a Malha, nor a Kalka a Kalka, but the young men of the one family chose their wives from among the young women of the other. Originally the Sanseeas confined themselves to mendicancy, minstrelsy, and cattle-lifting, but after a time, emboldened by poverty or impunity, they took to Dacoitee, which they reduced to a regular system.

In their expeditions they left their old men and women, and their children at home, under the protection of a friendly Zemindar, but took with them a few young women and such as had children at the breast, with a view to avert suspicion. When they arrived within two days' march of the scene of their projected operations, the main body halted, while the leader with a small party of followers, male and female, went on to reconnoitre and make the necessary preparations. Their usual plan was to enter a liquor shop, and while purchasing some spirits, to ask the name of some respectable money-changer or banker. They thus learnt the address of the one who was esteemed the wealthiest. On the following morning at early dawn they repaired to his shop, because at that hour he would be obliged to go to his treasure-chest, whereas, later in the day he would have a small supply of money beside him for ordinary business. Having now ascertained where his hoard was deposited, and such other particulars as might be useful, they proceeded to the bazar and procured a sufficient quantity of bamboos for spear-staves. These they buried near the town on their way back to the camp. All things being ready they took some spirituous liquor and spilling a little on the ground, prayed aloud: "O Davee! Mother! If we succeed in our business and get a good deal of booty, we will make a grand *poojah* (religious festival) to thee, and offer thee a cocoa-nut!" The goddess being propitiated, the next step was to assign to every man his particular post: some to act as scouts, others to guard the avenues, others again to rush into the house, while the Jemadar, or leader, reserved to himself the task of breaking open the money-chest with his trusty hatchet. Early next morning they advanced to an easy distance of the place, and some of them went forward for the spear-staves buried on the previous day. A Sanseea, of approved tact and intelligence again entered the town to purchase oil for the torches, and to make the final reconnoissance. So soon as darkness descended, the gang threw off their clothes and started at a rapid pace, without once looking behind. If they had reason to expect that the local police would be vigilant — a rare occurrence — they concealed their spears in a bundle of reeds or coarse straw, which one of them carried on his head, followed by another to personate the purchaser of the fodder. On arriving in front of the shop, the bundle was thrown on the ground, the cord hastily loosened, the spears extracted and the torches lighted. Then the Jemadar invoked the aid of his patron deity and vowed a grateful offering if the chest should at once yield to his blows. Raising their war-cry *Deen! Deen!* they furiously assaulted the bystanders, pelting them with stones, striking them with their spears, and even wounding them if obstinate. The Jemadar, the torch-bearers, and four or five determined men, under favour of the tumult, broke into the house, smashing doors and all other impediments. In a few minutes afterwards the house was abandoned by the unwelcome intruders, who moved off to the place of rendezvous as fast as their weighty plunder would permit them; the Jemadar piously imploring of Bhugwan to send their pursuers in a wrong direction. Should one of the gang happen to have been slain, his spirit was likewise invoked, and spirituous liquor and a goat promised to his manes. At every temple on the road, and at every stream they had to cross, they threw down a rupee or two to propitiate the genius of the place. When within a couple of miles of their encampment they called aloud Koo-Koo. If no response were heard they pushed on rapidly, occasionally imitating the call of the partridge: when close at hand they uttered a hissing noise. On their actual arrival they were certain to find everything packed up and ready for a start. Mounted on their rough, hardy little ponies they would cover a distance of sixty to eighty miles in twenty-four hours for two or three consecutive days, until fairly beyond all danger of pursuit. Any one was allowed to join a gang on payment of a few rupees, though not to carry a spear or enter the house until his coolness and courage had been freely tested. If a Dacoit committed homicide he was obliged to expiate his blood-guiltiness by making a *poojah*, at which he trusted his comrades with half a crown's worth of liquor. In the division of spoils the Jemadar claimed one-tenth in addition to the repayment of his advances towards fitting out the expedition. The balance was then divided among the entire gang, the leader again sharing, and provision was made for the wounded and for the widows of those who had fallen.

The religious creed of the Sanseeas was sufficiently simple. "I believe" said one of them, "in Ram (God), Bhowanee, and Sheik Fureed, whose shrine is at Gierur, about eighteen miles from Hingunghat. There we make offerings after a successful expedition. Sheikh Fureed acquired his saintship thus :—he first performed a devotional penance of twelve years, carrying about with him a load of wood tied to his stomach, but that was not accepted: next another, in which he ate nothing but forest leaves for twelve years —not accepted: lastly, his third trip, he hung himself up by the heels in iron chains in a Baolee (a well) at Gierur; then he was taken up and asked what he wanted; he said, to have every request granted; this was promised, and he disappeared. Many people now pray to him for luck."

Like the Thugs and the other Dacoits, the

Sanseeas prided themselves on the exact observance of omens. They looked upon it as unfortunate to hear the cry of the jackal or the cat, a kite screaming while sitting on a tree, the braying of an ass, a flute, or the lamentation over the dead. It was equally inauspicious to see a dog run away with any one's food, a woman break a water-pitcher, a hare, a wolf, a fox, a chamelion, an oil-vender, a carpenter, a blacksmith, two cows tied together, or a thief in custody. If they encountered a corpse, or if a turban fell off, or the Jemadar forgot to put some bread in his waist-belt, or left his spear or axe behind him—the expedition must be deferred. But nothing could be more promising than to meet a woman selling milk, or any one carrying a bag of money, or a basket of grain, or fish, or a pitcher of water. Nor was it less encouraging to see a calf sucking, or a pig, or a blue jay, or a marriage procession.

Their most binding form of attestation was by means of a piece of new cotton cloth, exactly 1¼ cubit square, in which was tied up half-a-pound of coarse sugar. The accuser hung the parcel upon the branch of a peepul tree, and challenged the accused to touch it. If the latter foreswore himself, he would sicken within three days. Another ordeal was to tie seven peepul leaves, one over the other, on the palm of the suspected person's hand, on which a red-hot iron plate was then placed. Unless he carried this seven paces without suffering any inconvenience and deposited it upon seven thorns arranged to receive it, he was pronounced guilty. At other times a Punchayut, or Council of Elders, seated themselves on the bank of a river, when one of them stepped forward and fired two arrows together from one bow, the one in the name of Bhugwan, the other in that of the Punchayut. The furthest one was then stuck upright in the ground, while a man walked into the stream up to his breast and planted a bamboo in the channel. The accused also entered the water and laid hold of the pole. A member of the Punchayut having clapped his hands seven times as a signal for him to plunge his head under the water, set off at the top of his speed for the arrow, brought it back, and again clapped his hands seven times. If the accused had kept his head immersed until this second signal, he was deemed innocent: otherwise, his guilt was held to be satisfactorily proven.

When a male child was born, his head was carefully shaved, with the exception of a small spot dedicated to Bhugwan. This lock of hair was all that he was permitted to wear until the completion of his tenth or twelfth year, when it also was shorn off by the barber, and his relatives gave a grand entertainment to the tribe. Those who died before this ceremony were simply buried with the face downwards: the only solemnity being the preparation of some sweet cakes, of which three were given to a dog and the rest consumed by relatives and friends. But those who survived this important epoch of their lives were, after death, placed on a funeral pyre. When the fire was extinguished, the ashes were carefully examined and the bones buried on the spot. Great feasting and jollity then followed, and the spirit of the deceased, propitiated by an offering of swines' flesh and spirits, was invoked to aid and protect his family.

Matrimony was a matter of arrangement between the parents; a Punchayut deciding the amount of the dower to be given by the father of the bridegroom to the bride's father. The marriage ceremony consisted in a libation of spirits to Bhugwan, the Supreme Being, and a public declaration that the boy and girl were henceforth man and wife; the whole concluding with a feast. If a man happened to be touched by the petticoat of his mother-in-law, or daughter-in-law, he lost caste, and therefore took care never to go near them. The same result was the consequence of his being struck by his wife's petticoat in the course of connubial strife. By thus losing caste he was incapacitated from joining his tribe in worship, or in funeral rites, though he was still allowed to eat and drink with them. However, a handsome entertainment to his brother robbers and a humble offering to the gods removed all impurities, social and religious.

The Bolarum Dacoitee committed in 1837 is such an excellent illustration of the system adopted by the Sanseeas that no apology need be offered for the length of the narrative, as given to Captain Malcolm ten years afterwards by one of the Dacoits actually engaged in it.

"From this place (Sadaseopath) I and four others came on to Hyderabad, where we looked about us for five days, but finding nothing likely to suit our purpose, we went to Bolarum, and took up our quarters at a buneeya's (tradesman's) shop in the village of Alwal, close to the cantonments. In the cantonments we soon discovered a respectable looking shop, which appeared well suited for a Dacoitee. Early one morning I took fifty shuhr-chelnee rupees with me and went to the shop, where I found the owner transacting business. I asked him to exchange the shuhr-chelnee for bagh-chelnee rupees, and when I had agreed to give him one pice discount on each rupee, he went and unlocked one of two large-sized boxes, which I saw in an inner room, and out of which he took the money I required. I also noticed some silver horse-furniture hanging upon a peg on the wall, and in a niche a dagger and a pair of pistols." "Having thus obtained all the information I required as to the exact spot where the property was likely to be found, I next examined the position of the different guards likely to interrupt us in the act of breaking into the house. I found that a guard of eighteen men was stationed at the chowrie (police station) some distance off, and that a sentry was posted at night at a place where four streets met, close to the shop I had reconnoitred. From the latter I feared no opposition, as he could easily be overpowered, and we calculated upon breaking into the house before the chowrie-guard could turn out and come to the rescue of the banker."

"I then returned to my comrades, with whom I remained for two days, making ourselves acquainted with all the localities about the place, the roads leading from it, and in fact with everything that might be of use to us in the enterprise we were about to undertake. Among other things, we learnt that after gun-fire, or eight o'clock, the guard had orders to stop all parties entering the cantonments, and we therefore determined to commence operations before that hour."

"We then returned to Sadaseopath (forty miles distant), and on relating the result of our proceedings to the gang, it was determined to risk a Dacoitee on the Sowar's house at Bolarum. Our next proceeding was to convey as secretly as possible to the vicinity of that place sufficient arms and axes to answer our purpose; these were made up into bundles and entrusted to four men, who proceeded in the night time to Puttuncherroo, and on the following night, a couple of hours before daybreak, we reached a small nullah (ravine) behind the mosque near Bolarum, where the axes and spears were carefully buried in the sand. The rest of our party in the meantime struck their camp, and, leaving the high road, made to the village of Tillapoor, about eight or nine miles from the fort of Golcondah."

"The gang chosen for the Dacoitee consisted of twenty-four able men, under Rungelah Jemadar and myself, and left Tillapoor about ten o'clock in the forenoon, and, in small parties of two and three, reached at twilight the spot where our arms were concealed. We then procured some oil from the shop in the cantonments, and, about half-past seven or nearly eight o'clock, we proceeded in straggling order towards the shop about to be attacked, and which we reached without being challenged by any one. The sentry posted near the shop we were about to attack did not appear to suspect or notice us; and the moment our *mussal* (torch) was lighted, he was speared by Baraham Shah and Kistniah, while others commenced breaking in the doors of the inner room, the outer partition of the shop having been found open. Three bankers, whom we found writing their accounts in the outer shop, rushed into the house and disappeared. The lock of the door yielded to one blow from the axe of Rungelah, and, on throwing down the planks of which it was formed, we found the box which I had seen on a former occasion, unlocked and open. Out of this we took sixteen bags full of money, leaving four, which we were obliged to relinquish, as we were pressed for time, and had not sufficient men at hand to remove them. The whole place now was in a state of commotion and uproar; and, as we drew off as fast as we could, we were followed by a crowd of camp-followers and Sipahees, to the place where a number of bullocks were picketed. We here struck into the paddy (rice) fields, and across these our pursuers did not attempt to follow us. A short distance from Bolarum, two of the bags broke, and the money fell to the ground; and as it was dark, and we had no time to search for it, we lost nearly 1,500 rupees." Nevertheless, they got off with 14,500 rupees, and with silver horse-furniture valued at £15 more.

The impossibility of guarding against these organized attacks by large bodies of armed men, through the means of the ordinary police, induced Lord Auckland in 1838 to appoint Captain Sleeman commissioner for the suppression of Dacoitee, in addition to his duties as General Superintendent of measures for the suppression of Thuggee. The task was a difficult one. Not only were the Dacoits protected and screened by the native princes, land owners, and magistrates—their own numbers and determination rendered their apprehension a matter of some danger. It was afterwards ascertained that in 1839 there were no fewer than seventy-two leaders south of the Jumna who could gather together 1,625 followers; and to the north of that river forty-six leaders, supported by 1,445 men. In the Oude jungles were many powerful colonies, who were usually warned by friendly Zemindars of the approach of danger, and thus enabled to flee to less accessible fastnesses. On one occasion 1,500 of them escaped into Nepaul where they temporarily dispersed, to meet again at a given rendezvous. The Commissioner himself aptly compared their colonies to a ball of quicksilver, which, if pressed by the finger, will divide into many smaller globules, all certain to come together again and cohere as firmly as before. However, the constant alarms to which they were now subjected, compelled them to conceal themselves in such unhealthy spots that they were decimated by disease. In the Goruckpore district a gang, consisting of ninety-four men and 280 women and children, suffered so much from this cause that they voluntarily surrendered themselves. Others were hunted down from one district to another, until in despair they yielded themselves prisoners, or endeavoured to abandon their illegal vocation and settle down to agricultural pursuits. Many of the prisoners, being conditionally pardoned, were admitted into the police force, where they distinguished themselves by their courage and intelligence. It is a remarkable trait in the character of the Dacoits that they rarely forfeited their word. If once they pledged themselves not to revert to their former evil habits, there was little danger of a relapse. An experimental colony was formed of the approvers and their families near Moradabad, at a place called, *de nomine facti*, Buddukabad. The result has been satisfactory, though the Dacoits usually complained of the difficulty of confining their expenditure to the comparatively small means furnished by honest industry. A Budduk, they would say, cannot live on eight rupees a month (three rupees being the wages of an ordinary labourer): he requires at least two rupees a day, because he eats meat and takes large quantities of *ghee* and rice, and loves liquor, and is addicted to polygamy. One of them, who had been ten years in prison, being asked by Capt. Ramsay if, in the event of his liberation, he would promise to amend his life, shook his head and answered with a merry laugh:—"No, no, that would never do. Why should I become an honest man—work hard all day in the sun, rain, and all weathers, and earn—what? Some five or six pice a day! We Dacoits lead very comfortable and agreeable lives. When from home, which is generally only during the cold season, we march some fourteen or sixteen miles a-day for, perhaps, a couple of months, or say four, at the outside—commit a

Dacoitee and bring home money sufficient to keep us comfortable for a year, or perhaps two. When at home we amuse ourselves by shooting, or visiting our friends, or in any way most agreeable—eat when we please, and sleep when we please—can, what you call an honest man, do that?"

Another who had passed a like period within the gaol at Lucknow, returned to Dacoitee a few months after his release. "I was then young," said he, "and in high spirits—I had been confined with many other old Dacoits— and in gaol I used to hear them talking of their excursions, how they got 50,000 rupees here and 20,000 rupees there; and I used to long for my release, that I might go on Dacoitee and enjoy myself." The confessions of both these men would be readily endorsed by many inmates of our own prisons. Evil associations and the charms of a contraband career are equally potent in Europe and in Asia. But among the natives of India the profession of a Dacoit was not regarded as one of shame and disgrace. Indeed, even the Commissioner avowed he could see little difference, ethically, between expeditions in quest of plunder, and those for the purpose of conquest; it was a question of degree, not of principle.

They themselves gloried in their calling. "Ours," they said, "has been a *Padshahee Kam* (an imperial business); we have attached and seized boldly the thousands and hundreds of thousands that we have freely and nobly spent: we have been all our lives wallowing in wealth and basking in freedom, and find it hard to manage with a few copper pice a day we get from you." So energetic, however, and persevering were the measures adopted for the suppression of this "Padshahee Kam" that within a very few years after their inauguration, there existed in the Upper Provinces scarcely even the nucleus of a gang. The few who still remained at liberty were known by name and personal appearance, and only escaped apprehension by leading simple and inoffensive lives, gaining their daily bread by their daily labour.

The task of suppression in the Lower Provinces has been attended with so many peculiar difficulties, from the natural configuration of the country, that Dacoitee can hardly yet be said to be extinguished. But its days are numbered, and a marked diminution of cases is observable every year. The apathy of their victims has, undoubtedly, been one great cause of the impunity so long enjoyed by these daring marauders.

This reluctance to prosecute, though partly owing to a well founded dread of incurring the vengeance of the comrades of convicted Dacoits, is chiefly attributable to the repugnance felt by all respectable natives to appear in Court even as complainants. The tedious formalities of legal proceedings appear to them in the light of studied annoyances, and their dignity is offended by the distrust with which their statements are necessarily received. Perhaps, the ancient mode of administering justice would be, after all, the most efficacious, and certainly most in accordance with the native character. The elders of the town, or village, seated at the gate, or beneath the grateful shade of stately trees, and presided over by an English gentleman conversant with their habits and language, and possessed of tact, patience, and good sense, would probably dispense more even-handed justice than is obtained by all the costly paraphernalia of courts of law founded on a totally different phase of civilization. Be this as it may, enough has now been said to disprove the vulgar allegation of indifference to the welfare of their fellow subjects so flippantly and frequently urged against the Government of the East India Company. And these are only two out of many instances that might be adduced to show that their administration has been one of continued and consistent progress. It is reserved for posterity to admire the gratitude that seeks to reward the annexation and improvement of a vast empire by maligning the motives of those to whom this country is indebted for the brightest gem in the imperial crown, vilipending their services, and depriving them of power and patronage.

The Mangs.

Some curious and interesting information has been furnished by Captain C. Barr, of the Bombay Native Infantry, with regard to the Mangs, or Kholapore Dacoits. It is needless to observe, that Kholapore was one of the early divisions of the Mahratta empire, or that it separated from the main body in 1729, under the auspices of one of the younger branches of Sivajee's family. The Mangs occupied the very lowest grade in the ladder of society—or, rather, they were looked upon as outcasts, and quite beyond the pale of society. They harboured in wilds and forests, and lived upon carrion, roots, and wild fruits. Their real occupation, however, was that of border robbers; and yet it was a source of pride among them that their wives should remain ignorant of the nature of their pursuits. They never robbed or defrauded one another; they even believed that the spoliation of "the Gentiles" necessitated an expiation, which usually assumed the form of a gift of a pair of shoes to a Brahman, and alms to the poor. Experience had taught them the expediency of employing a peculiar dialect—perhaps it was the original language of their race. Their leader, or headman, was called the Naïk, and was selected by the majority of votes for his skill in planning an expedition, his bravery in carrying it out, and his integrity in the division of the spoils. The office was, consequently, not hereditary; but they so far believed in the efficacy of blood, as to allow considerable weight for a father's merits. The Naïk's person and property were alike inviolable. On all ceremonial occasions his precedence was allowed; in disputes, his decision was final; and on him devolved the duty of laying out plans for robberies. To every band was attached an informer, who was also the receiver of the stolen goods. These scoundrels generally pretended to be, and perhaps were, bangle-sellers, dealers in perfume, goldsmiths, jewellers, &c., &c. In this capacity they were admitted into women's apartments, and so enabled to form a correct notion of the topography of a house, and a shrewd guess as to the wealth of its inmates. Their mode of conducting a Dacoitee was in all respects similar to those already described. The only persons exempt from their depredations were bangle-sellers and agricultural labourers, who, in return, afforded them refuge and hospitality in the hour of need. After a successful foray, each of the gang contributed one-fourth of his share to the Naïk, towards the common fund for defraying the expenses of preparation, absolution, and feasts of triumph. The informer was not entitled to any specific sum; but, as he enjoyed the privilege of pre-emption of the booty, his interests are not likely to have been overlooked.

Like all barbarous tribes, and all persons addicted to criminal practices, the Mangs were extremely superstitious. They never, for instance, set out upon an expedition on a Friday. The new-born child was bathed in a spot previously prepared for the purpose, and baptized by the Brahman, in the name of the deity presiding over that particular hour. In the family, however, and throughout life, the neophyte sinner was known by some household name. Danger was encountered at an early period of life. The mother and another woman stood on opposite sides of the cradle, and the former tossed her child to the other, commending it to the mercy of Jee Gopal, and waited to receive it back in like manner, in the name of Jee Govind.

The Mangs usually married young in life. If a girl happened to hang heavy on hand, she was married, at the age of puberty, to the deity. In other words, she was attached as a prostitute to the temple of the god Khundoba, or the goddess Yellania. Those belonging to the service of the latter were wont, in the month of February, to parade the streets in a state of utter nudity. It was customary, previous to a secular marriage, for the parents of the bridegroom to ask for the hand of the bride. A test of the aspirant's address was then demanded. In one instance, the father of the maiden filled a silver vessel with water up to the brim after carefully suspending it over his head in bed, so that the slightest touch would be certain to splash the water on to his face. The suitor, however, was not daunted by the difficulty of the enterprise. Procuring some dry porous earth, he employed it as a sponge, carefully applying it to the surface of the water. Having thus reduced the level of the surface, he cut the strings, carried off the vessel, and next morning claimed his bride. The marriage ceremonies were by no means interesting, except when a bachelor wooed a widow. In this case he was first united to the *asclepias gigantea*, which was immediately transplanted. Withering away and dying, it left him at liberty to marry the charming widow. If a lady survived the sorrow caused by the death of two or three husbands, she could not again enter the holy state unless she consented to be married with a fowl under her armpit—the unfortunate bird being afterwards killed to appease the manes of her former consorts.

Each family had its household god, but all agreed in the common worship of Davee, as the tutelar deity of the tribe. Their chief festival was the Dusserah, on which day they usually set out on their expeditions, armed with sword and shield, and iron crowbar. Unhappily, the Mangs must be spoken of in the past tense. The servants of the East India Company, actuated, no doubt, by mercenary motives, have put an end to their depredations and compelled them to resort to honest and common-place industry. Thus are sentimentality and romance crushed at the India House.

The Oothaeegeerahs,

OR

Professional Thieves.

In the year 1851 it was accidentally discovered that the British territories had long been infested with gangs of thieves from the Banpoor States. These Sunoreahs, or Oothaeegeerahs, who extended their depredations into the very heart of Calcutta, had carried on their vocation with impunity for many generations. Their existence was well known, however, to the native authorities, from whom they received protection and encouragement. The head man of each village was *ex officio* chief of the Sunoreahs, and kept a registry of the various "nals," or gangs under his own jurisdiction—usually from seven to ten in number. In Tehree they were estimated at 4,000, in Banpoor at 300, and in Dutteeah also at 300. There were in all twelve villages occupied by them, presided over by a Government officer, whose duty it was to act as umpire in all disputes arising out of the division of spoils.

Shortly after the Dusserah festival the chiefs

of each village repaired to their favourite Brahman priest to ascertain in what direction they were to bend their steps. This having been duly indicated, together with the auspicious day and hour, they started off in a body to some place of considerable note. Here the gang, consisting, probably, of fifty or sixty men, was subdivided into parties of ten or twelve, and detached to adjacent towns and villages, while the leader, with a strong party, remained at the point of separation. Hither they all returned in the month of July; and, if their joint exertions had produced fifty or sixty rupees for each man, they then hastened home to prepare their fields for the summer crop. But should fortune have proved unfavourable they again took to the road, while their leader alone hastened back to the village laden with plunder for their respective families. The office of Mookeea, or leader, was hereditary, and, in default of male issue, descended to females. If among the booty there happened to be any object of peculiar elegance or value, it was ceremoniously presented to the chief of the state. Thus, the head of the Tehree Government acknowledged a present of two valuable pearl nose ornaments, by bestowing on the thief a grant of land, rent free, in perpetuity;

and the Rajah of Banpore was known to have accepted two handsome watches and a pair of arm ornaments. There was no mystery in the disposal of their stolen goods. These were openly sold in the market places and bazaars at half their value, and, during the absence of the Sunoreahs on their thieving expeditions, the village money-lender unhesitatingly supplied their families with whatever they might require. Of course, care was taken never to commit any depredations within the territories of their protectors and patrons.

The Sunoreahs had "chounees," or depôts in all parts of India, where they could always find a ready sale for their effects. Near Calcutta their head quarters were at the serai of the Rajah of Burdwan, whose ostentatious hospitality oftentimes maintained as many as 200 of them. Though usually possessed of ample means, they never scrupled to accept alms with the Byragees, or religious mendicants at Burdwan. No matter how widely they might have roamed from their native villages, they always found ready purchasers for their pilferings, and they themselves easily recognised each other by means of a peculiar "bolee," or slang.

When their proceedings first became known to

Major P. Harris, Superintendent of Chundeyree, that officer immediately addressed the Rajah of Banpoor on the subject, and elicited from him a most naïve and characteristic reply, the following extract from which well exemplifies the native notions of morality and good government:—

"I have to state that from former times these people following their profession, have resided in my territory and in the states of other native princes; and they have always followed this calling, but no former kings, or princes or authority have ever forbidden the practice; therefore these people for generations have resided in my territory and the states of other princes; proceeding to distant districts, to follow their occupation, robbing by day for a livelihood for themselves and families, both cash, and any other property they could lay hands on. In consequence of these people stealing by day only, and that they do not take life, or distress any person, by personal ill-usage, and that they do not break into houses, by digging wells or breaking door-locks, but simply by their smartness manage to abstract property; owing to such trifling thefts I looked on their proceedings as petty thefts, and have not interfered with them. As many States as there may be in India, under the protection of the British Government, there is not one in which these people are not to be found, and it is possible that in all other States who protect them, the same system is pursued towards them as in my district; and besides, these people thieving only by day, the police officers in the British territories are not expected to exert themselves, the loss having occurred simply through the owner's negligence. Owing to this circumstance, your friend looking on their transgressions as trifling, I have not caused my police to interfere with them. The British Government, who issue orders to all the native powers in India, have never directed the system of Sunoreahs to be stopped. From this I conclude that their offence is looked upon by the British Government, as trifling; and probably this is the reason that neither the British Government, nor any other authority, have ever directed me to stop their calling; and on this account, from property that they have brought home, and I have heard that it suited me, or that they themselves, considering the article to be a curiosity from a distant province, have presented to me through my servants; thus, viewing the offence as trifling, that there was no owner to the property, I received it from them, and gave them a trifle in return."